SPEAKING OF ETHNOGRAPHY

MICHAEL H. AGAR
University of Maryland

Qualitative Research Methods,
Volume 2

SAGE PUBLICATIONS
The Publishers of Professional Social Science
Beverly Hills London New Delhi

Printed in the United States of America

For information address:

SAGE Publications, Inc.
275 South Beverly Drive
Beverly Hills, California 90212

SAGE Publications India Pvt. Ltd.
M-32 Market
Greater Kailash I
New Delhi 110 048, India

SAGE Publications Ltd
28 Banner Street
London EC1Y 8QE
England

International Standard Book Number 0-8039-2561-1
0-8039-2492-5 (pbk.)

Library of Congress Catalog Card No. 85-050781

SECOND PRINTING, 1987

When citing a University Paper, please use the proper form. Remember to cite the correct Sage University Paper series title and include the paper number. One of the following formats can be adapted (depending on the style manual used):

(1) AGAR, MICHAEL H. (1985) Speaking of Ethnography. Sage University Paper series on Qualitative Research Methods, Volume 2. Beverly Hills, CA: Sage.

or

(2) Agar, Michael H. 1985. *Speaking of ethnography*. Sage University Paper series on Qualitative Research Methods (Vol. 2). Beverly Hills, CA: Sage.

CONTENTS

SERIES INTRODUCTION

Contrast and irony provide the definitional context for this series of monographs on qualitative methods. Contrast is inevitable because the label itself makes sense only when set against something it is not. Irony is also inevitable as the denotative contrast between the qualitative and quantitative is so often misleading, if not downright false. The mandate for the series is then paradoxical. We wish to highlight the distinctions between methods thought to be qualitative and quantitative, but also to demonstrate that such distinctions typically break down when subject to scrutiny. Alongside the Sage series on Quantitative Applications in the Social Sciences comes the Sage series on Qualitative Research Methods, but the wise reader had best intermingle the monographs of the two sets rather than stack them on separate shelves.

One way of approaching the paradox is to think of qualitative methods as procedures for counting to one. Deciding what is to count as a unit of analysis is fundamentally an interpretive issue requiring judgment and choice. It is, however, a choice that cuts to the core of qualitative methods—where meanings rather than frequencies assume paramount significance. Qualitative work is blatantly interpretative; but, as the work in this series demonstrates, there are a number of increasingly sophisticated procedures to guide the interpretive acts of social researchers.

The monographs in this series go beyond the short confessionals usually found in the methodology sections of research reports. They also go beyond the rather flat, programmatic treatments afforded qualitative methods in most research textbooks. Not only are qualitative methods becoming more variegated, going well beyond the traditional look, listen, and learn dicta issued by traditional field researchers, they are also being shaped more distinctly by explicit philosophical and moral positions. This series seeks to elaborate both qualitative techniques and the intellectual grounds on which they stand.

The series is designed for the novice eager to learn about specific modes of social inquiry as well as for the veteran researcher curious about the widening range of social science methods. Each contribution extends the boundaries of methodological discourse, but not at the expense of losing the uninitiated. The aim is to minimize jargon, make analytic premises visible, provide concrete examples, and limit the scope of each volume with precision and restraint. These are, to be sure, introductory monographs, but each allows for the development of a lively research theme with subtlety, detail, and illustration. To a large extent, each monograph deals with the specific ways qualitative researchers establish norms and justify their craft. We think the time is right to display the rather remarkable growth of qualitative methods in both number and reflective consideration. We are confident that readers of this series will agree.

—John Van Maanen
Peter K. Manning
Marc L. Miller

EDITORS' INTRODUCTION

There are many ways qualitative researchers define their respective tasks. Michael Agar, in this second contribution to the Qualitative Research Methods series, embeds his aims within a natural language perspective, finding that the central research problem is akin to the problem of communication. In many ways, Professor Agar's approach to ethnography differs considerably from that of Professors Kirk and Miller in Volume 1. It directly challenges the assumed usefulness of conventional scientific procedures as the appropriate models for the study of human affairs. *Speaking of Ethnography* is informed by a hermeneutic and phenomenological tradition and puts the researcher's own taken-for-granted procedures of knowledge acquisition at the center of the research process. That these procedures are open to inspection and therefore subject to critical assessment is perhaps the fundamental thrust of this monograph. Taken together, Volumes 1 and 2 are analogous to conceptual bookends marking distinct and antagonistic perspectives on just how the social world can and should be studied.

PREFACE

This book was put together at the invitation of editors John Van Maanen, Peter Manning, and Marc Miller for the new Sage series on Qualitative Research Methods. It consists in large part of revised versions of material that appeared in previous articles and chapters. I am grateful to the following sources for permission to use that material: *American Anthropologist* ("Toward an Ethnographic Language," 1982, Vol. 84: 779-795); *Human Studies* ("Inference and Schema: An Ethnographic View," 1983, Vol. 6: 53-66); *Urban Life* ("Ethnographic Evidence," 1983, Vol. 12: 32-48); and the University of Illinois Press ("Growing Schemas out of Interviews," with Jerry Hobbs, in *Cognition in Action*, edited by Janet Dougherty, 1985). Other material is taken from a book manuscript I'm working on, *Independents Declared,* forthcoming from Smithsonian Institution Press.

I am also grateful for three as yet unpublished manuscripts that take seriously the ideas from the earlier articles. They are cited in the book. They are (in the order in which I received them) an elaborate critique of the arguments by Jerry Kirk and Marc Miller, an application of those ideas by Tony Whitehead, and a second application by Ann McElroy and Mary Ann Jezewski. I was complimented by, and learned much from, their work.

Speaking of Ethnography has its roots in a book I did on ethnography called *The Professional Stranger* (1980). That book was planned as a readable introduction to ethnographic research, one that gave some general feel for it without getting lost in technical detail. But I finished the project wanting more of just that—technical detail. Fortunately, at that time I had the benefit of a Career Development Award from the National Institute on Drug Abuse. The award gave me a few years of freedom to read and write around the issues. During the time spent at the University of California, Berkeley, I also had the chance to try some things out in seminars, as well as to work with Jerry Hobbs of the Artificial Intelligence Center at SRI International. Although some of our collaboration is referred to in the book, many of the ideas developed here were joint productions in our discussions.

At the University of Maryland, John Caughy in American Studies provided helpful comments, as did the Sage series editors, especially Marc Miller. Lori Spier helped out with the final preparation of the manuscript. Many hours of conversation with ethno-friends Linda Bennett and Erve Chambers contributed in too many ways to try to figure out. But the final product, as the saying goes, is my problem.

SPEAKING OF ETHNOGRAPHY

MICHAEL H. AGAR
University of Maryland

1. INTRODUCTION

When professional social researchers set out to investigate the human situation, a way of thinking about and describing their work travels with them. It doesn't matter if they are interested in juvenile delinquents, Indian villagers, corporate decision making, Dublin poets, or the relationship between SAT score and astrological sign. Whenever two researchers meet, they can talk about their research by using a *common language*, one in which they can propose their work, discuss it as it progresses, or evaluate its results.

The problem is that there are different styles of social research but only one dominant language to talk about them. The dominant language is sometimes called the "received view" of science, a view that centers on the systematic test of explicit hypotheses. I don't plan to describe the received view in its entirety here, and as I assume that readers of this book *are*—or are in training to be—professional social researchers, such a description is unnecessary. No one really believes that the received view describes how *all* social research is done. But when grants and articles are reviewed, when research is discussed in panels or over dinner, inertia has a way of rearing its ugly head. "What's your hypothesis?" "How do you measure that?" "How large is your sample?" "Did you pretest the instrument?" "Did you use discriminant function analysis?" So goes the litany of questions that the received view generates.

For some social research styles, especially those that emphasize the *scientific testing role*, those questions make sense. But for other styles—when the social researcher assumes a *learning role*—the questions don't work. When you stand on the edge of a village and watch the noise and motion, you wonder, "Who are these people and what are they doing?" When you read a news story about the discontent of young lawyers with their profession, you wonder, "What is going on here?" Hypotheses, measurement, samples, and instruments are the wrong guidelines. Instead, you need to learn about a world you don't understand by encountering it firsthand and making some sense out of it.

The social research style that emphasizes encountering alien worlds and making sense of them is called *ethnography*, or "folk description." Ethnographers set out to show how social action in one world makes sense from the point of view of another. Such work requires an intensive personal involvement, an abandonment of traditional scientific control, an improvisational style to meet situations not of the researcher's making, and an ability to learn from a long series of mistakes. The language of the received view of science just doesn't fit the details of the research process very well if you are doing ethnography.

In the past this lack of fit only caused a sense of embarrassment in discussions with self-appointed "real" scientists. At present, as ethnography is used increasingly in a number of fields, there are other consequences. Now we have self-appointed "ethnographers" producing superficial studies, as well as competent ethnographers who are unable to account for their understanding of others. Ethnographers need a language to describe and evaluate their research, one that better represents the way it actually works. This book proposes the outlines of just such a language. More broadly, the series in which this book appears explores a variety of them.

But *Speaking of Ethnography* is hardly the first one to make the attempt. Garfinkel (1967) built much of ethnomethodology to address the gap between the received view and the study of how ordinary folks accomplish their everyday lives. Geertz's *The Interpretation of Cultures* (1973) and Goffman's *Frame Analysis* (1974) also set forth well-written perspectives on the study of social life that set out to do the same job. But none of them quite work. They are too partial, too narrow in focus, and too detached from ethnographic practice.

To start our quest for a more general, more practical ethnographic language, we should first examine some of the classic differences between ethnographic research and the evaluative standards of the received view. There are many, but an examination of a few that are often mentioned will demonstrate the need for an ethnographic language.

Some Ethnographic "Problems"

In the field of anthropology, examples abound that demonstrate how different people produce different studies. For instance, no sooner did George Peter Murdock develop the Human Relations Area Files (HRAF) than the blemishes appeared. Comparative work yielded a number of interesting problems, among them the difficulty of comparing different ethnographic reports that were supposedly about the "same" thing. Descriptions of child rearing, for example, might vary depending on the professional training of the ethnographer—Freudian psychology, learning theory, or an interest in kinship would all lead to different descriptions. As a result, partial accounts are difficult to compare. The problem is more acute when personal as well as professional issues are considered. Devereaux (1967) describes the effects of one's *personal* history on social research. The title of his book, *From Anxiety to Method in the Behavioral Sciences*, sums up the argument.

Another example of how different ethnographers produce different research is found in the discussion of restudies. Lewis and Redfield provided the classic case, and Derek Freeman's criticism (1983) of Margaret Mead is the most public and recent example. But several cases exist that show how two researchers came up with descriptions of "the same" group that differed in important ways (see Naroll, 1970, for a review). Another volume in this series (Kirk and Miller, 1985) treats the problem elaborately in terms of reliability and validity.

The restudy problem becomes more interesting when the two ethnographers are of different cultures. There are a few early cases around, such as Li An Che's article on the Zuni (1937). But with the increase in the number of Third World ethnographers, we will see more and more critiques of Euroamerican ethnography in the future. (See Owusu's 1978 discussion of African ethnography for an example.) In fact, recent issues of *Current Anthropology* reflect the growth of what is called indigenous anthropology. In these discussions, we learn that ethnographies can differ because of different cultural backgrounds of ethnographers, sometimes in ways that bring to light implicit Western assumptions buried within anthropology.

A particularly striking demonstration of the importance of cultural differences occurred at the International Congress of Anthropological and Ethnological Sciences in New Delhi. European and American anthropologists were criticized by Indian members of the audience for sorting behaviors into "sacred" and "secular." To understand Indian village life, they argued, one had to realize that "religion" was involved in most situations of daily life. Sorting events into sacred and secular destroyed the phenomenon before it could be analyzed. If "our" culture did not lead us to emphasize this distinction, they claimed, we would better understand our problems in Iran. (The meeting was held in December 1978, a time when the United States was flabbergasted at how easily a "sacred" leader took over a "secular" society.)

There are reasons other than differences among ethnographers that help us understand why two studies might differ. For example, the group described may change. In my own work, initially conducted in a treatment center for heroin addicts in the late 1960s, I described some of the knowledge needed to understand the subculture of heroin addicts. When I began work in the mid-1970s, I was struck by the changes taking place as heroin availability dramatically declined while that of methadone increased (1977). Heroin addict activities had altered in response to changes in the chemical ecology of the streets. The descriptions changed partly because the group was truly different. Many other examples show such differences when an ethnographer revisits a group after some period of time (Mead, 1956; Foster et al., 1978).

Ethnographies may also differ because of the intended audience of an ethnographic report. In my own work the presentation of the same chunk of ethnographic material takes different forms depending on whether I write for clinicians, drug policymakers, survey sociologists, or cognitive anthropologists. Anthropology as a field is just beginning to define this as a disciplinewide problem.

In traditional academic anthropology, ethnographers write for a limited audience consisting of scholars much like themselves. With their similar training and cultural backgrounds, the traditions of ethnographer and audience overlap. In contrast, when an ethnographer's intended audience consists of different readers, new constraints are added that limit the forms that the research can take. When one's audience includes, say, psychiatrists in a medical school, agency bureaucrats, or members of a community, new problems arise. One need only scan recent issues of *Human Organization* and *Practicing Anthropology* to see this new awareness and the thoughts it has inspired.

To sum all this up, ethnographies of similar groups, or on similar topics, differ one from another. They differ because of differences in the audiences addressed, in the background of the ethnographers, or even in the groups themselves. But that does not exhaust the problems ethnographers have when they come up against the received view. An item of folklore holds that anthropologists are (in)famous at granting agencies for proposing one study and returning with another. Barrett (1976) describes how he went through four economic models as his fieldwork progressed. The fourth model differed significantly from the first one, the one he originally proposed to test. Glaser and Strauss (1967) explicitly show the importance of the *emergence* and *revision* of analytical categories in ethnographic work as part of their "grounded theory" approach. Needless to say, this emergence is dissonant with the received view of social research that describes linear movement from hypothesis through data collection to analysis.

Then there is the problem of emphasizing the *understanding* of situations that have occurred rather than the *prediction* of the value of one variable given the knowledge of the values of others. Like linguists, ethnographers are less interested in knowing exactly what comes next and more taken with understanding what just occurred. You cannot possibly know what to do next unless you know what just happened, goes the argument. This understanding occurs in a variety of ways, although all of them involve a connection between something said or done and some larger pattern. The pattern may involve links to actors' intentions, to conventions of group life, or to both in some combination.

Ethnographic studies come up with different results; they don't know where they are going to end up; they don't predict the future. "What good are they?" comes the question from the received view. One answer to the question—an answer currently pursued by many anthropologists—is to make as much of ethnography as possible fit the received view. I think that is a mistake. Another answer is to argue that ethnography is a different research style with different strengths. The problem is that the received view cannot talk about it. A different language is required.

At this point a couple of stories are in order, stories that illustrate some typical ethnographic data as problems in understanding. Along the way, the key concept of tradition will come up as a way to characterize the encounter among ethnographer, group, and perhaps an audience with a tradition partially distinct from both.

Tradition and Ethnography

The first story comes from the old-fashioned type of anthropological fieldwork. Some years ago, while working in South India, I was preparing to leave at midday to visit another village a few miles distant. As the cook fixed my lunch, he placed a small lump of the charcoal on top of the food just before wrapping a cloth around it. I was bewildered. I could not make sense of his act. Later, I learned that I was traveling at a time when spirits were particularly active, and because spirits are further attracted by food, the charcoal was placed on top as a spirit repellent. Any child in the village knew about that.

Some years later I lectured to a class at the University of Puerto Rico, using the example to illustrate the process of fieldwork. At the end of the lecture, the professor and two of the students told me they were surprised that I had been so surprised. As soon as they heard the story, they said, they assumed it had something to do with spirits. I remembered readings I had done on *espiritistas* and *santerias*, the spiritual healers found in some Puerto Rican and other cultural groups. Apparently their background better prepared them for a coherent sense of the villagers' use of charcoal.

The next story comes from some anthropological work on the analysis of a heroin addict's life history (Agar and Hobbs, 1985). In one interview, Jack (as we call him) describes a situation in Penn Station in New York. He is sitting in the station to keep out of the winter weather when a young "cat" comes up and asks him to keep his eye on his luggage while he "makes the john." Jack describes how he did not intend to steal the luggage, but another street type sitting nearby insisted on going through the bags and sharing what was there. Jack refused, took the bags, and left the station.

When "straight" listeners hear this story, there is no problem in understanding it. But when I explain that the surprising thing about the story is that Jack hesitated at all, the expectations that guided their understanding crumble. By street rules, anyone who is foolish enough to be separated from his property is a "lame," a "mark." It is now automatic that the property is fair game. By commenting on his hesitation and reporting that he stole the luggage only because he was forced to, Jack is acknowledging the straight world addressed in the interview while still reporting an outcome that is normal in the street world and is the backdrop for the story.

These two examples show the importance of the different *traditions* that make up an ethnographic encounter. Tradition is simply a shorthand term for the resources available to make sense out of experience. The charcoal did not make sense in my tradition; I had to modify and connect it with the tradition of the Indian villagers. Jack's story easily makes sense from a viewpoint inside your tradition. I had to show you that another tradition exists that also serves as a resource to make sense of his story, but show you in a way that preserves the connection between Jack's tradition and yours.

An ethnography is first of all a function of the ethnographer, who brings to his or her work the tradition in which he or she participates, including the training received in professional socialization. The kinds of events that present themselves as problems are partly a function of how sensible and how coherent they are, given that tradition. The charcoal immediately created problems for my understanding of a normal village event; apparently a Puerto Rican ethnographer would have had less difficulty.

Ethnographies are also a function of the group among whom the ethnographer is working. If the village cook had not placed a lump of charcoal in the package, I would have just carried it off onto the trail without another thought. If the heroin addicts among whom I had worked had not often talked of "beating" and "burning" people, I would not have asked the questions and made the observations that suggested the nonstraight interpretation of this small piece of Jack's life history.

Ethnographies also depend on the nature of the audience. The ethnographer is trying to produce a report for somebody else, to show how the life of some group makes sense. If the audience participates in the same tradition as the ethnographer, then the ethnographer only needs to make his or her personal understanding explicit. However, in the Indian village example, I apparently overexplained the charcoal incident for the Puerto Rican audience. On the other hand, with the story of stealing the luggage, straight audiences have to be shown that a different understanding *is* possible. They easily make sense of the story from within their own tradition; they must be shown that the story has an additional sense, one that they were originally unaware of.

To sum all this up, ethnographies emerge out of a relationship among the traditions of ethnographer, group, and intended audience. Ethnography is at its core a process of "mediating frames of meaning" (Giddens, 1976). The nature of a particular mediation will depend on the nature of the traditions that are in contact during fieldwork.

The received view's concept of "objectivity" becomes obsolete. Ethnography no longer claims to describe a reality accessible by anyone using the right methods, independent of the historical or cultural context of the act of describing. On the other hand, there is no justification for the complete relativism of what Hirsch (1976) calls "cognitive atheism" either. There is a human group out there who lived in a world before the ethnographer appeared and who will continue to do so after he or she leaves. The research is a function of the group studied as well.

Ethnographer, intended audience, and group all represent traditions that limit, but do not fully determine, the possible ethnographic reports that can emerge. Ethnography is neither subjective nor objective. It is interpretive, mediating two worlds through a third.

2. ETHNOGRAPHIC UNDERSTANDING

When the different traditions are in contact, an ethnographer focuses on the *differences* that appear. Expectations are not met; something does not make sense; one's assumption of perfect coherence is violated. For convenience, the differences noticed by an ethnographer are called *breakdowns*. The term is Heidegger's, though the general idea is illustrated in a variety of anthropological discussions. Sperber (1974), for instance, writes that those actions noted for their symbolic interest are precisely those that are marked departures from what the ethnographer expects.

Rosenblatt documented several other examples of a focus on breakdowns: "If one looks at descriptions by anthropologists of their field experiences, it seems quite common that the initial reaction included comparison embodied in surprise or attention to the unexpected" (1981: 199). He notes that Naroll and Naroll (1963) also mention the "attention to the exotic," although they characterize it negatively as a bias. Rosenblatt mentions several ethnographic accounts that support his point (Nakane, 1975; Uchendu, 1970; Pandey, 1975; Gould, 1975; Mohring, 1980). He also writes that some anthropologists "advise one to use surprise, the unexpected, or a sense of difference as cues to what to study" (1981: 200), and cites Levine (1970), Mead (1970), and Richards (1939) to support his point.

Such examples from the literature (not to mention the anecdotes from my own work) illustrate the central role of breakdowns in bringing out problems for ethnographic attention. A breakdown signals a disjunction among the traditions; the problem for ethnography is to give an account that eliminates it. The *specific* nature of the breakdown will be a function of the traditions of ethnographer, group, and audience. Change any of the three and the content of the breakdown may change too. The definitive ethnography does not exist.

Once a breakdown occurs, something must be done about it. For convenience, we will call the process of moving from breakdown to understanding a process of *resolution*. The process is an emergent one; and like the breakdown that triggers it, it is constrained by the traditions in which it occurs. One way to think about resolution is by way of analogy with Hirsch's (1976) notion of the "corrigible schema." A breakdown is a lack of fit between one's encounter with a tradition and the schema-guided expectations by which one organizes experience. One then modifies the schemas or constructs new ones and tries again. Based on this new try, further modifications are made, the process continuing iteratively until the breakdown is resolved.

Another version of resolution is found in the work of the philosopher Hans Georg Gadamer (1975). He writes that a tradition has a boundary—the limits of its point of view—called its horizon. Resolution occurs when the horizons of the different traditions have been "fused"—changed and extended so that the breakdown disappears. Gadamer's version of resolution is well illustrated in Rabinow's personal account of fieldwork in Morocco (1977). He takes us through several encounters that produced breakdowns and then shows us how the resolution was worked out.

According to Gadamer, resolution is a linguistic/conceptual *process*. Language is the public storehouse of tradition, the signal of just what it is in the world that is significant, the resource for speculatively creating new worlds. So it is no surprise that he concludes that the fusion of horizons is the "proper achievement of language" (1975: 340). When we combine the importance of language with resolution's dialectic, emergent nature, we see resolution as a process that relies on a logic of question and answer. With the exception of Collingwood's work (1978), little has been done on this kind of logic since Socratic dialogues.

There is no method to generate good questions in a mechanical way; they arise within the encounter of different traditions, inspiring sequences of questions and answers that emerge dialectically until the breakdown is resolved. An anthropological version of this view of resolution can be found in the recently collected works of Charles Frake (1981). To reinterpret his work into the current framework, his earlier papers show the importance of linked questions and answers as a means to the end of "schema correction." The later papers criticize those who saw in the earlier arguments a mechanical method, and then recast the question/answer logic back into the general problem of doing ethnography in a manner parallel to that of Gadamer.

Once resolution is complete, Gadamer says that the details of the process disappear. Once a breakdown is resolved, it leaves our conscious attention. For ethnography, we will have to document resolution on some selected basis so that we can make our case. Michael Moerman (1969) identified this problem some time ago. As fieldwork progresses, an ethnographer becomes less reflective about earlier encounters. The informants also become less informative because they assume the ethnographer knows more. The same issue arose when a filmmaker presented her work to the Anthropological Society of Washington. She reported that the ethnographer, who had been in the field for some time, was enthusiastic about the film crew's presence because their questions and observations brought back some of the key concerns he had had when fieldwork began, concerns forgotten with time. Translated into the present discussion, ethnographers had successfully resolved early breakdowns and then lost consciousness of them. Fine, if you're a philosopher; a problem if you're an ethnographer.

Breakdown is the starting point and resolution is the process it initiates. How does the process end? The end point is called *coherence*. A coherent resolution will (1) show why it is better than other resolutions that can be imagined; (2) tie a particular resolution in with the broader knowledge that constitutes a tradition; and (3) clarify and enlighten, eliciting an "aha" reaction from the members of different traditions that make up the ethnographic encounter. A successful resolution will also do more than resolve a single breakdown. The coherence that results must apply in subsequent situations. To use Winch's (1958) phrase, understanding must proceed "as a matter of course."

So far some core vocabulary for an ethnographic language has been introduced. In an encounter of different traditions, a breakdown occurs. Resolution begins with an openness to new possibilities, and leads to a dialectic process of question and answer until the traditions have been linked. The original departure from expectations is now seen as coherent. Whatever else ethnography is, it is in part a movement from breakdown through resolution to coherence. In the next three sections, each of the notions—breakdown, resolution, and coherence—are described in more detail. Coherence first.

Coherence

Schutz, an interpretive philosopher concerned with the nature of understanding in social research, devoted much time to the problem of coherence. To summarize his position in his own words, "It suffices, therefore, that I can reduce the other's act to its typical motive, including their reference to typical situations, typical ends, typical means, etc." (1970: 180). Behind this summary, needless to say, lie some elaborate arguments. We will now turn to them in order to begin to develop an ethnographic version of coherence.

A person, living in a world endowed with meaning, has at any given moment an interest at hand. For our purposes, this interest at hand will be called a *goal*, of which the person may or may not be conscious. The goal of the moment is not an isolated entity; rather, it is part of a larger system of goals in the person's world. Some goals lead to an intention to bring about some state of affairs in the world. These are of particular interest for ethnography as it is the publicly expressed action of informants that is the source of breakdowns and resolutions.

Before discussing Schutz's version of coherence, his analysis of the different temporal perspectives on action must be outlined. "Action" is the lived experience of the actor at the time of its doing. An "act", on the other hand, is a reflectively contemplated action. One can only know one's actions as acts because to contemplate them is to step outside of them. If an action is imagined as it might be done in the future, it is a "projected" act. The first step toward coherence lies in an appreciation of how this projection is accomplished.

The actor, with goal at hand, sketches out a plan of action based on anticipations and expectations in the stock of knowledge available. The knowledge is organized around the goal in terms of the degree of its relevance. Grosz (1978) calls this goal-directed attention to knowledge a matter of *focus*. A goal, then, brings different parts of knowledge into greater or lesser focus. Schutz notes that an intention to bring about the goal (the "in-order-to" motive) will readily focus knowledge if the situation is a familiar one. If it is not, our actor may have to go up a level and solve them before projecting. Schutz also notes that the knowledge must be clear and consistent "enough" given the goal, but with decreasing focus these requirements relax.

The actor's stock of knowledge is primarily organized into typifications; we will use the modern term *frame* instead (Minsky, 1975). Frames develop, according to Schutz, when the experience of one object is transferred to any other similar object (1970: 117). Frames are generalized "knowledge structures" that have "empty places" and "variables" that are "filled in" with the details in particular instances of their use (Schutz, 1970: 130). Many of them are encoded in language. In fact, Schutz characterizes language as a "treasure house" of frames—one that carries the tradition across the biographical situation of different actors. He also notes that frames change with experience; the actual carrying out of a project will "enlarge and restructure them" (1970: 142).

With Schutz's thoughts translated into the modern terminology of knowledge representation, we have a way to talk about coherence. The observer imagines what the in-order-to motive of the actor might have been, given observation of an act, and then projects his or her own "fancied carrying out of such an action as a scheme in which to interpret the other's lived experiences" (Schutz, 1970: 177). For an observer, coherence is achieved when an actor's expression (performed with or without communicative intent) is seen as part of a larger project, or what we will now call a *plan*. Coherence, in short, is achieved by giving an account of an act in terms of its relations to goals, frames in focus, or both as they interrelate in a plan. And that is simply a summary in contemporary terminology of Schutz's conception, quoted at the beginning of this section.

From Schutz we get an elaborate description of coherence. It requires the reflective examination of action as act, whether distantly observed or shared as lived experience with informants. The act is coherent if it fits into a plan that we imagine it might have been a part of, where plan is a cover term for an organization of goals and frames. Ethnographic coherence, in brief, is achieved when an initial breakdown is resolved by changing the knowledge in the ethnographer's tradition so that the breakdown is now reinterpreted as an expression of some part of a plan.

Breakdown

From the end of the resolution process we now return to the beginning—the breakdown that initiated it. Anticipating later discussions of the complexities of actual fieldwork, I would like to do some concept splitting. These splits do not precisely sort breakdown experiences. Rather, they help one understand the emergent nature of ethnographic work.

The first distinction separates *occasioned* and *mandated* breakdowns. When I worked in South India, I had no idea that I was going to have to make sense of a lump of charcoal in my lunch pack. It came up, surprised me with its apparent lack of sense, and presented itself as a problem in understanding. It was occasioned. On the other hand, when I heard junkies using the terms "beat" and "burn," I knew that as a linguistic anthropologist one of my key tasks was to put them into the lexicon. The focus on terms, the conscious attention I directed toward them, and the kinds of sense I began to make of them were mandated.

Mandated breakdowns are those that you set out to create. Occasioned breakdowns are those that come up unexpectedly when doing an ethnography. The difference is primarily whether or not the breakdown was intended by the ethnographer. The two are not independent in actual ethnographic work, but the distinction is a worthy one. It accounts for the common ethnographic experience of setting out with a mandated breakdown and returning with some occasioned ones that prove more interesting.

Mandated breakdowns are also worth distinguishing for two other reasons. First, traditional hypothesis-testing methods of social research are in fact attempts to mandate breakdowns; an ethnographic language should include those methods as well. Second, the idea of mandated breakdowns encourages questioning one's understanding of situations as a general principle, a particularly important stance when working in one's own culture. (Later in the book, the discussion of anticoherence will flesh this out.)

Breakdowns can also be distinguished by whether they are *core* or *derivative*. Core breakdowns are the main focus of an ethnographer's work and eventual report. Derivative breakdowns are less important. They may be seen as such simply because of time limits, or because within the ethnographer's tradition they are so evaluated, or because they are only handled incidentally on the way to resolution of core breakdowns. Some breakdowns are top-level problems for an ethnographer; others come up but are dealt with less thoroughly.

To exemplify the distinctions, let me return to my two examples. The encounter with the charcoal was derivative and occasioned. In South India, the core breakdown that I focused on was the relationship between social groups and leadership in conflict resolution. This was, in turn, occasioned rather than mandated, although in retrospect it obviously responded to my faculty audience, who were interested in that particular theoretical problem.

In the junkie example, the attempt to learn about "burn" and "beat" was mandated and core. My training as a linguistic anthropologist emphasized the careful attention to lexemes as a primary inroad to culture. The process of working out what those terms meant was derivative, but was both mandated and occasioned. It was mandated because I used ways of forcing breakdowns suggested by then current elicitation methods in ethnosemantics; but it was also occasioned as the use of the terms by myself and others, and observations of referents identified by the terms, created further problems.

Not all breakdowns are the same. At one extreme, an ethnographer may set out to force a breakdown and spend much time resolving it—it is mandated and core. At the other extreme, unexpected breakdowns may come up and receive little attention—they are occasioned and derivative. However, it is one of the special strengths of ethnography that a breakdown that was originally mandated disappears or may become derivative, while something that came up serendipitously as an occasioned breakdown may move to the center and become core.

Resolution

Now that the beginning and end points are defined, the resolution process that moves from one to another can be dealt with. First we need a general way to talk about the pieces of a tradition in terms of which encounters are or are not understood. In the discussion of coherence, the notions of goals, frames, and plans were introduced. The modern term *schema* serves as a cover term for all three. (All these terms—goal, frame, plan, and schema—are currently in vogue in several academic disciplines. I'm using them because they refine our understanding of how knowledge *changes*, and knowledge change is what resolution is all about. Later in this book, the sources of these terms are more elaborately discussed.)

When a breakdown occurs, we have a schema problem. Now we need a term for the diverse phenomena used as data in ethnographic work. The term *strip*, as introduced by Goffman (1974) and used by Frake (1981), will serve the purpose. A strip might be an observed social act, recognized as a unit by the nature of its characterization in the informants' language. It might also

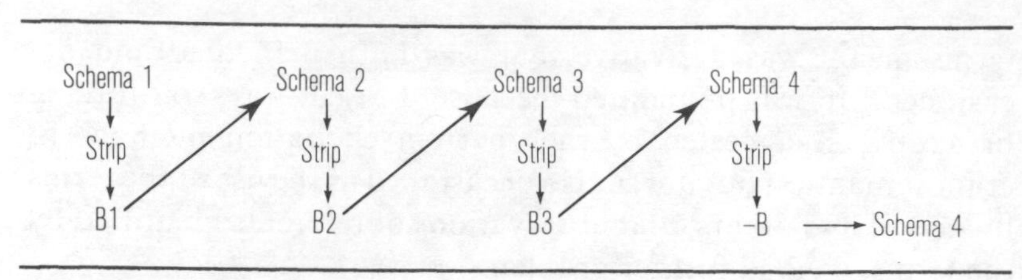

Figure 1 Single-Strip Resolution

be an informal interview conducted by an ethnographer, or a more structured interview or experiment. It could also be a document of some sort. In short, a strip is any bounded phenomenon against which an ethnographer tests his or her understanding.

Resolution, as a process, works through the repeated application of schemas to strips. When strips are understood with available schemas, there is no breakdown (although an ethnographer may try to mandate one, as discussed later in the section on anticoherence). When a strip is *not* understood, a breakdown occurs and resolution is called for.

The simplest type of resolution is summarized in Figure 1. Some schema, labeled "Schema 1" in the figure, applied to some strip, produces a breakdown, labeled "B1." The ethnographer modifies the schema, leading to the new Schema 2. It in turn is applied to the same strip, but another breakdown—B2—occurs. Further modifications in the schema lead to Schema 3. The process iterates through repeated modifications of the schema and applications of the strip until no breakdown occurs. In Figure 1, this is indicated by the "–B," leading the ethnographer to accept Schema 4 as coherent for the strip.

The "single-strip" resolution of Figure 1 is at the heart of ethnographic work. But schemas must work with more than just one strip. Ensuring that they do is called multiple-strip resolution, depicted in Figure 2. For the sake of continuity with Figure 1, Figure 2 begins with the Schema 4 that finished up the earlier resolution. The resolution begins with a second strip, labeled "Strip 2" in the figure.

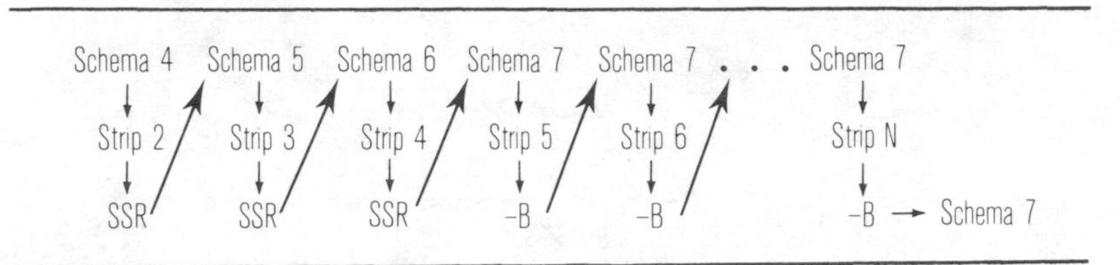

Figure 2 Multiple-Strip Resolution

Figure 2 begins with the straightforward application of Schema 4 to Strip 2. A breakdown occurs, so (just as in Figure 1) the arrow in the diagram moves back up to the schema. But this time the arrow is labeled with an "SSR" rather than with a "B." "SSR" is just an abbreviation for the resolution already described in Figure 1—single-strip resolution. Figure 1 is collapsed into Figure 2. When a breakdown occurs in the application of the schema to a new strip, the single-strip resolution process is used until that breakdown is resolved.

Once that is taken care of, there is a new schema, Schema 5. This in turn is applied to a new strip, Strip 3, and the process continues iteratively just as it did in Figure 1. But there is a difference in how the process terminates. In Figure 2, Schema 7 produces no breakdown when applied to Strip 5. The process does not stop there. Instead, Schema 7 is applied to several more strips, 7 through n, until we are *sure* that no further breakdowns will occur.

How do we know when we are sure? When is n large enough? The general idea is that we stop when no further breakdowns come up in encounters with additional strips. But there are problems here. First, breakdowns can occur later in the research against schemas thought to be coherent. Second, the sampling of strips in ethnography is one of the enduring problems of method. The problem isn't resolved here; the point is that the language highlights it, as it should.

I want to introduce one more type of resolution, one that is central to the ethnographic emphasis on holism (Phillips, 1976). As schemas are modified in single- and multiple-strip resolutions,

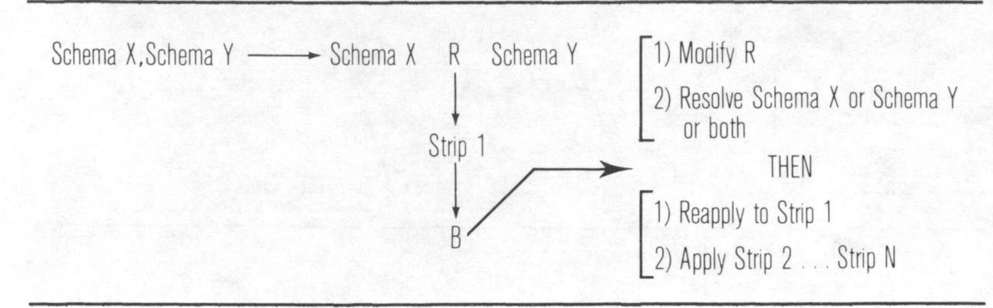

Figure 3 Schema Resolution

ethnographers typically wonder if the modifications form some interesting pattern across schemas. They seek what Gregory Bateson calls "the pattern that connects." Sieber (1973) points out that this emphasis carries with it the danger of the "holistic fallacy." By this he means a tendency to overemphasize integration at the expense of conflict and disharmony. It is for just this reason that a more careful look at what we will call schema resolution is called for.

The process of schema resolution is depicted in Figure 3. The figure begins at the left with two schemas, Schema X and Schema Y. A holistic view leads one to wonder about interconnections between the two. The ways that schemas might be interconnected are numerous. For example, I might have an intuition that two schemas are related because one schema represents an event whose outcome is a prerequisite for the event represented in the second schema. (I used this relationship in my earlier ethnographic work with heroin addicts. One outcome of "copping," or buying, heroin was obviously heroin, which in turn was a prerequisite for "getting off," or injecting it.)

Figure 3 shows that there may be a relationship (like the prerequisite-outcome link) between Schema X and Schema Y. The relation, indicated with the symbol "R," is shown in Figure 3 as "Schema X R Schema Y." Just as in the earlier resolutions the related schemas are applied to a strip; a breakdown occurs. In contrast to the first two processes of resolution, however, a number of remedies are possible.

The holistic fallacy is one possibility, but assume we are not willing to accept that yet. One possible modification lies in the relationship R. Perhaps outcome-prerequisite isn't quite right; maybe the two schemas are related in some other way. (Maybe one event "causes" the other, for example.) Or we might suspect that the resolution of the two schemas together brought out problems in one or both of them that did not appear when they were resolved individually. In that case, we could use single- or multiple-strip resolutions on one or both of them before trying schema resolution again. After modifications are made, the new form of "Schema X R Schema Y" is reapplied to the same strip or applied to new strips, as noted in Figure 3. The resolution would proceed iteratively, just as it did in the simpler forms already discussed.

Schema resolution is critical for ethnography, which emphasizes the development of higher-order schemas that show the relations among several lower-order ones. This push to higher levels represents the continuing effort to come up with an articulate statement of our sense of group concerns that are so pervasive, so fundamental, that they appear in numerous situations and across many social relations. We can't get there with a list of schemas; instead, the list must be transformed into a pattern.

Real fieldwork is not, of course, so easy. Among other things, it is more complicated in the number of strips dealt with, the number of schemas under consideration, and the many levels at which resolution proceeds. This partly explains why fieldwork is so intellectually exhausting. Then, in addition to all this simultaneous iteration of the process, it can also be maddeningly recursive. A breakdown occurs and resolution begins, which in turn produces a derivative breakdown, so the process is put on hold while resolution of that begins; but a new derivative breakdown appears, and so on. To extend the adage, it's easy to get lost in the trees.

Notice also that nothing in this discussion holds that resolution necessarily determines a schema uniquely, nor does it argue that schema modifications come only from a single source—theory, informant statements, observations, and intuitions can all provide ideas. At the same time, resolution does require that schemas—whatever their source and eventual form—be anchored in the strips we abstract out for study from group life. It is this commitment to strips that gives ethnography its "emic" flavor, and it is in the possibility of applying schemas across a wide range of strips that validation strategies will be developed later in this book. Before dealing with ethnographic evidence, however, a clearer sense of this business of tinkering with schemas is called for. And before schemas are discussed, some background on the concept of inference is also required.

Inference and Schema

Inference is a word that calls to mind elegant formal systems such as Euclidean geometry or first-order predicate calculus. Inference only occurs in those systems if you follow strict rules, but the rules are guaranteed to work. If you start out with some truths and apply the rules of inference, then whatever you wind up with is a truth as well. If you know that "A and B" as a single concept is true, then you automatically know that "A" and "B" are true individually. If you know that "A→B" is true, and you also know that "A" is true, then "B" must be true as well.

The problem is that neither geometry and logic nor their formal cousins are flexible enough to help with ethnographic resolution. Many who talk about knowledge and reasoning do strive—with good reason—for the simple elegance of traditional formal systems, the mathematical pinnacle of certain knowledge and the goal of "received view" science. But if we stick to traditional logic as the evaluative standard, we are put in the position of dismissing most inferences as deviant, faulty, or not up to the standard (Tyler, 1979).

Why do we need the concept of inference at all? From an ethnographic point of view, inferences are nothing less than the glue of coherence. They link different pieces of knowledge and connect knowledge with the world. Whenever I assert that if I know or observe one thing then I know another thing, I have made an inference. For the present we need to explore inference, but the exploration does not carry with it an effort to cast ethnography into the formal attire of first-order predicate calculus. Quite the contrary.

First of all, the kinds of knowledge linked by our inferences can be of a variety of sorts. Situations, persons, objects, actions, and goals can be connected in whatever way a particular problem in understanding calls for. The connections are much richer than the traditional ones available in classic formal systems. Besides, inferences can come in bunches; in fact, one reason why the concept of schema was developed in the first place was to articulate the different kinds of bunching that occur. Once one has a sense that a situation is of a certain type, or a person is in pursuit of a particular goal, inferences lead away from that knowledge to a wealth of knowledge connected to it.

Inferences also may be uncertain. In classic formalisms one thing always implies something else, and that's that. In contrast, recent work recognizes "plausible" inferences, as introduced in the work of Polya (1954) and developed by Collins (1975, 1978). Does changing the oil guarantee that your car won't blow up? Well, no, but it tends to prevent it. To further complicate matters, plausibility itself comes in several strengths. From A we may possibly, or sometimes, or usually, or almost always infer B.

Then in addition to the plausibility of the inference, there may be "hedges" on the As and Bs and links that constitute them (Kempton, 1978). If you are polite to the boss, will she give you a raise? Well, maybe you weren't polite enough; or maybe she isn't exactly the boss; or maybe you got a new typewriter, which is "sort of" a raise. Hedges and plausibility further loosen the notion.

We have already come some distance from formal logic, leaving the rarified air of certain truth for a better fit with our intuitions about the kinds of new schemas an ethnographer constructs to resolve breakdowns. But we are still left with a concept—inference—that forces us to pay attention to what sort of knowledge we are linking up in our work and in what sort of way we do so.

Much recent work in artificial intelligence (Hobbs, 1978; Rieger, 1975), psychology (Collins, 1975, 1978), and anthropology (Colby et al., 1981; Colby and Colby, 1981; Hutchins, 1980) moves toward the identification of looser systems of inference. Typically, a list of distinct inference types is offered. We will not concern ourselves at the moment with evaluating the completeness of the lists, but we will take in the more general points: (1) Making sense is accomplished by linking up some expressed act with a lot of knowledge, which is itself interlinked. (2) Two pieces of knowledge (including knowledge from observation), together with the link that connects them, constitute an inference. (3) Inferences may be both plausible, in the sense of their certainty, and hedged, in the sense of how well they apply to an instance of attempted sense-making. (4) Inferences will have a content that comes from the traditions of understander and act to be understood, but (5) at the same time the form of the inferences may pattern in a way that eventually leads us in the direction of a more general theory.

From an ethnographic point of view, we are interested in inferences as a way to give more systematic shape to the resolutions that we use to make sense of action. The break with traditional formal systems has led to a potpourri of discrete types. To begin to move toward a more coherent view, we first need a better sense of what inferences are.

To begin in one standard way, we can discuss inferences in terms of *nodes* and *links*, where nodes are the things connected and links are the things that do the connecting. Nodes may be states, actions, persons, goals, or objects. The simplest type of inference works by asserting a link of an unspecified nature between one node and any other. Further, the inference may be constructed on the basis of presence or absence, absolute or hedged, of either node type.

A few examples: (1) "What's he doing pouring whiskey in his tea? He thinks he's W. C. Fields." Sense is made with a simple action-person inference. Or, perhaps, "He has a cold." In this case, we have an action-state inference. Or, "He wants to get drunk"—action-goal. Or, "We always put whiskey in our tea"—action-object. Or, "So he can serve it to his friend"—action-action. These inferences all involve the presence of both nodes; similar examples could be constructed using different mixes of presence and absence. For example, "He's out of rum" would be action-lack of object.

Things get more interesting when the nature of the link is also specified. Two nodes may be tied together because one causes the other, or enables it, or results in it, or evaluates it, or is part of it, or is a token of it, or resembles it, or co-occurs with it in space-time. On the one hand, the link may be expressed in a simple linguistic form—"Whiskey cures colds," "Whiskey gets you drunk," "Whiskey is like rum," "Whiskey is good for you," or "Whoever heard of tea without whiskey?" Again, the links could deal with absence rather than presence—"Whiskey won't hurt you," for example.

More typical will be cases where the inferences come in groups. They group because some inferences will share nodes or links with others. "He's putting whiskey in the tea because he wants to get drunk. Alcohol does that, and whiskey is alcohol. He had a rough day at the office, and he usually gets drunk after a rough day." As mentioned earlier, this bunching of inferences is what the term "schema" is all about. The usual ethnographic case involves schemas rather than single inferences.

To summarize so far, the concept of inference represents the idea of linking up knowledge, whether constituted from memory or from interaction with the world. Inferences are made up of nodes and the link or links that ties them together. They may be asserted with varying degrees of plausibility or hedging, and may involve either presence or absence of the phenomena to which they are matched. Nodes may be actions, states, persons, goals, or objects. In their simplest form, inferences simply assert a link between any two. In their more complex form, the link itself is specified. Usually an inference used to make sense of some act will be tied together with others, giving rise to a schema.

This discussion of inference and schema gives a sense of what they are and how they work. (There are similar discussions, such as Schank and Abelson's [1977].) It also gives us a handle on the idea of an ethnographic resolution of breakdowns. Breakdowns occur when available schemas, either serendipitously or through forced analytic effort, fail to make sense of action. Resolution is the process of tinkering with inferences and schemas until coherent understanding is achieved.

Strips

Now that schema and inference are a little more rounded out, the same can be done for strips. Ethnography is experientially rich. Out of all the experiences that an ethnographer has with informants, some portion of them are abstracted out for careful study. Ethnography is notorious for dealing with different kinds of strips—observation, conversation, interview, archive, or literary text might all contribute strips to the resolution of a particular breakdown.

Strips may differ from one another in a variety of ways—on the dimension of *control*, for example. At one extreme, their form and content are primarily under the ethnographer's control; at the other, the strip is under the control of group members. Ethnography is unique in emphasizing the importance of this second kind of strip. It is committed to making sense out of the way the folks naturally talk and act when they are doing ordinary activities. Some argue that the researcher's presence necessarily alters the informants' world, and of course that's often true. But sometimes we overrate our impact. After a period of time, one becomes—sometimes—part of the woodwork. Besides, Becker

(1970) argues that group members live within well-established tradition that constrains their actions. The presence of an ethnographer is a new constraint, but it is in competition with many others that have the weight of tradition behind them.

At the other end of the control scale, an ethnographer might design a strip—a structured interview or experiment, for example. If the folks are willing to participate, they then enter into a situation that unfolds according to the ethnographer's plan. Actual strips will, of course, range all over this scale, but for now the two endpoints help characterize the differences.

A second type of variation among strips lies in the nature of the *record*. At one extreme, an ethnographer may participate in an event just to get the feel of things with no intention of recording it in any way. At the other extreme, an event might be preserved on videotape, enabling repeated viewing of the language and motion that constituted it. Just like the control issue, most strips will fall between these two extremes. For example, an ethnographer might set out to watch for a few things as he or she moves through different situations. Those few things, together with some minimal information about the context, then go into a written record. Such a recording strategy is obviously somewhere between the videotape and nothing at all.

A third type of variation lies in the *level* of the strip. At the first level are strips that are part of the informant's routine accomplishment of daily life. At the second level are strips that are constituted by discourse about those level-1 strips. At the third level are strips that consist of discourse about level-2 strips. While the levels could in principle expand upward forever, ethnographic work in practice seldom goes beyond level 3 (see Bruce, 1979, 1980, for a similar characterization of stories in terms of levels, as well as Goffman's [1974] concept of "lamination"). Notice that any strip at level N is also a strip a level N – X, where N > X > 0. For example, a level-2 strip can also be analyzed as a level-1 strip (e.g., an informant discussion about an event can also be seen as an accomplishment of everyday life).

An ethnographic example is available in the charcoal story. The cook placed a lump of charcoal in a lunch he packed for me when I left to walk to another village. The act occurred as a level 1 strip under group members' control. (In the rest of the discussion, "ethnographer" and "group member" control will be used to indicate a change in degree of control, rather than in the sense of absolute ends of the scale.) Assume that after I left the village, the cook and two other villagers talked about it—that would be level 2 (but also level 1). Then the cook leaves, and the two villagers talk about how excessively worried he was—that would be level 3 (although again it could be analyzed as 2 and 1 as well).

Or consider another version with more ethnographic control. After the charcoal is placed on the food, I initiate a move to level 2 by asking the cook and nearby villagers why the charcoal is there. Later, the cook tells me that what the villagers said was not to be believed; they were putting me on. That would be level 3. There might even be a level-4 strip, if one of the villagers overheard and later talked to me about how the cook told me that because he didn't want me to think villagers were superstitious.

Strip variation in level and degree of control helps characterize a strong ethnographic bias. We consider a large dose of level-1, folk-controlled strips to be the sine qua non of ethnography. Access to such strips is one reason for an ethnographer to be involved for a long period of time in the informant's home territory, not to mention his or her traditional concern with relationships high in rapport.

Experiments are ethnographically suspect because although they are level 1, they are researcher controlled. Surveys are suspect because they are both level 2 and researcher controlled. Ethnographic interviews standing alone are suspect because although they are more informant controlled, they are level 2. Microethnographies (of classrooms, clinics, and courtrooms, for example) are suspect because although they may contain level-1, informant-controlled strips, their range of coverage is too narrow. Ethnographers draw from strips that differ in level, degree of control, and recording strategy; but the emphasis on level-1 informant-controlled strips is central to our field. In my experience, when those strips are missing or limited, it is occasion for comment. It constitutes a breakdown in our schema for an ethnography.

3. BORROWED TERMS IN NEW CONTEXTS

The notions of inference, schema, and strips contribute some clarity to our sense of ethnography as a process of coherently resolving breakdowns. But many of the concepts used in previous sections—plan, goal, and frame as well as schema and inference—draw from fields such as artificial intelligence and cognitive science. In those fields, the concepts work in service of goals distinct from ethnography's. In cognitive science, for example, they are used to model human cognition, to build pictures of the mind that explain memory, problem solving, and decision making. In artificial intelligence, the concepts are used to guide the development of computer programs that enable the machine to do tasks requiring intelligence—tasks ranging from story understanding to advising an exploration geologist.

In ethnographic work, the primary goals are not modeling minds or programming computers. The goal is to resolve breakdowns, to build the new knowledge through which social action in one tradition can be seen as coherent from the point of view of another. Because of the change in goals, the concepts—schema and the others—are used in different ways. In the next few sections, some of the major differences are described.

Similarities

Ethnographers try to make sense of human differences in terms of human similarities. The emphasis is on *bridging* traditions—tinkering with inferences until action in one tradition is understood from the point of view of another (Becker, 1982). The focus is on differences; inferences and schemas are modified until understanding can occur. But an ethnography is not just a list of differences, for they must be made sense of in terms of similarities. At the same time, arguing that *all* similarities must be represented is a mistake—it opens up a bottomless pit. Differences, as they arise in breakdowns over the course of ethnographic work, are to be resolved. The question that remains is how and for what reasons one should discuss similarities as well.

The first problem is that no clear boundary between differences and similarities may exist. For example, when I was developing a lexicon during my study of heroin addicts, some terms were clearly group specific and therefore needed to be included; other terms were clearly mainstream American English and could safely be left out. But a few were marginal, making it hard to decide whether to include them or not. The marginality was made more difficult as my study was done in the late 1960s, when much street argot was moving into standard English. My strategy was to err on the side of caution and include a term if I thought there was any chance a potential reader would not know it. But the problem remains—sometimes the boundary will be unclear.

Similarities between traditions remain important, however. They are the ground against which the figure—the breakdown—appears and is resolved. Until now we have spoken of the "new knowledge" needed in one tradition in order to make sense out of the acts that occurred in another. But the "new," to borrow and extend Clark's (1975) notion, needs to be connected with the "given." Further, there may be degrees of newness. Some of the new may only involve minimal additions to or deletions from the knowledge already available. Other breakdowns may require changes that substantially reorganize the knowledge originally brought to the encounter.

As an example of minimal changes, consider the example of cooking food in a South Indian village. Early on, when I walked into a village hut in the evening, I had no trouble looking at the pots over the fires and deciding that cooking was going on. I had to replace some low-level schemas from my tradition, as electric or gas stoves and metal pans with handles were not being used, but on the whole the originals worked adequately for understanding.

Now for an example of more fundamental change, let's consider some research on the use of methadone in New York (1977). I had some knowledge from my work with addicts in the late 1960s, but when I began research in the city I experienced a new breakdown. I kept hearing people in the street talking about methadone, not as part of treatment but rather as a desirable new street narcotic.

The key to the resolution occurred when I noticed that with a schema substitution of methadone for heroin, many of the same lower-level schemas constructed in my earlier work served to interpret methadone-centered activities in New York in the 1970s. The culture change that had gone on was reflected in a core schema rather than in the many lower-level schemas to which it was linked. There were of course also important differences between the junk scene of the late sixties and the methadone scene of the early seventies. But it was only after the insight that the key was the high-level schema change that these differences became coherent.

These brief examples illustrate how schema changes that resolve ethnographic breakdowns can run from the minute to the fundamental. But whatever the magnitude of the changes, the point remains. The new knowledge must connect adequately with old knowledge available in the tradition of the ethnographer (not to mention the intended audience of a report). This connection occurs when the differences have been resolved so that they connect with similarities and allow a coherent understanding of a social act. At that point, further elaboration of similarities is unnecessary, as the ethnographer/audience can fill in the needed additional background.

Similarities among traditions also suggest a possible relationship with human universals. People everywhere have language. They all recognize the importance of such phenomena as sex, birth, human development, and death. They all live in physical worlds where seasonal variation, climate, the diurnal cycle, and astronomical phenomena will be noticed. People everywhere experience emotions, such as love, anger, fear, and happiness. The use of human universals as a similarity to link up differences is important in that they *guarantee* that any two traditions can be connected.

Returning to the South Indian village, suppose that I tell you about an instance of conflict and one of the lines in an interview I quote says, "Sakrya's older brother was angry with him for using the cart." I need to be sure that the reader knows that "brother" is used here in the sense of "father's male sibling's son" rather than in the sense of descendants of the same parents. And of course the "cart" issue is an important difference that will require some schema construction. But beyond that, I can be sure that any (English-speaking) reader will have a sense of brothers as kin and anger as a strong emotion. Anyone is capable of making sense of the statement because they share a common humanity with narrator and group.

Universal similarities are particularly crucial to an ethnographer. For any two traditions that one is attempting to bridge, universals offer a guaranteed link. It is interesting in this regard that some of the literature on field methods mentions the importance of "face-to-face" universals in the conduct of fieldwork (Powdermaker, 1966; Pelto and Pelto, 1973). One can also imagine that they are important in any group that is constituted cross-culturally, such as international business or diplomacy.

Similarities between traditions—specific or universal—are necessary to present a coherent report as well. An ethnographic report is a kind of discourse. Suppose I am giving you a sketch of a videotape of a wedding prior to analyzing it to show the new knowledge needed to make sense of it. "The groom wakes up at dawn. He gets up from his cot and walks over to the clothes-pole." Now, the new knowledge needed to understand this account isn't very interesting—people sleep on cots rather than beds. Houses contain clothes-poles of such and such a form, they don't have closets, and so on. Further, it is not particularly startling to point out that people wake up, stand up, and get dressed in the morning.

But in giving you a sense of a piece of social action that is going to serve as an anchor for the analysis of differences, coherence requires that certain things be said. Many of these things will represent areas of similarity between the two traditions. However, constraints imposed by the form of the ethnographic report require them to be present. A report has as its goal the presentation of new knowledge to readers or listeners. As such, it is a form of communication, and it is therefore subject to the constraints imposed by the form of communication chosen to do the job.

Finally, similarities may serve as the overall goal of an ethnographic study. One can set out to produce an ethnography that shows that group X is really not as different from the audience group as the audience group might think. The report emphasizes those aspects of group life that show how their concerns are the same as those of the audience; or, alternately, that given the social, physical, and biological environment anyone would be doing pretty much the same things. The point of such an ethnography, in other words, would be to elicit a breakdown in the audience.

Even without this intent, ethnographies often portray groups in a "sympathetic" light. The basic goal of showing that activities are coherent reduces the distance between audience and group. In the early pages of *Tally's Corner*, for example, Liebow (1967) sets up a situation where ghetto males are on a streetcorner. A white employer drives by looking for workers. When he calls out to them, none of the men respond, and the driver leaves with his views confirmed that black ghetto men don't want to work. Liebow then shows how, for each of the men, there are good reasons why they didn't respond—some of them, for example, had just gotten off work. The men have reasons for their lack of response—their act made sense. The use of similarities to bridge traditions usually reduces the distance between the traditions. When one reads an ethnography of a South Indian village and sees the villagers dealing with their children or harvesting the millet or planning for a forthcoming wedding, there is an ease of identification that brings them closer to the reader's own experience.

Whether as goal or consequence of the use of similarities to bridge traditions, ethnographies reduce distances between groups. One use of ethnography in complex societies is as a means of "humanizing" stereotypes. But many have also found in doing an ethnography that one may be criticized for being "overly sympathetic."

Similarities provide the ground for ethnography; differences, the figure. The inferences and schemas developed during the research will focus on the differences. The problem for an ethnographer is not to decide when a schema is "complete"; instead, he or she must decide when the differences have been resolved "enough" for understanding to take place.

The Outside and the Inside

A debate has been going on for years between those who emphasize "actor's meanings" and those who stress "observed" characteristics of the world—characteristics of which the actor may be unaware. One version of the argument in anthropology marches to the tune of emic and etic—the former emphasizing folk concepts and the latter stressing those of the ethnographer. Another version is found in the criticism of interpretive sociologies that they fail to account for power differences and institutions (Giddens, 1976). Yet another example lies in the debates between Gadamer and Habermas—Habermas arguing that language is but a part of the world; other parts, it is maintained, have more to do with "causes" of behavior and less to do with their "interpretation" (McCarthy, 1978).

Ethnography is committed to strips from group life as both a source of breakdowns and a test of their resolution. In this sense, it is always committed to emic phenomena. But when building schemas, raw material for construction comes from both the folk and the ethnographer. A group member might articulate a complex schema that makes sense of a strip; that schema can then be incorporated wholesale into the ethnography. An ethnographer might construct a schema based on bits and pieces that he or she has heard and seen, with a dash of insight and intuition. At the other extreme, an ethnographer might draw on some theory to construct a schema that has nothing to do with anything group members ever said, even though it is linked in explicit ways with strips that they performed.

In this section I want to consider how theory fits in with ethnographic resolutions. For ease of discussion, those schemas motivated by some theoretical position are called theory schemas (see Geertz's related discussion of "experience-distant" concepts [1976]). I would like to take two examples, with apologies for the oversimplified treatment of the theories they come from, and see what role social science theory schemas play in ethnographic understanding.

The two examples reflect two different relationships of theory schemas to resolution. On the one hand, they may be part of the newly won knowledge used to understand strips directly. On the other hand, theory schemas may take as their referent the schemas used in understanding, leading to the construction of higher-level knowledge. In principle we could expand even further. For example, one could demand schemas that are another level higher than the schemas that are a level higher than the schemas used in understanding strips—something like the domain of epistemology. But for now we will deal with the two lowest levels.

As an example of theory schemas with direct application, consider a single inference that comes from a clinical perspective on heroin addicts: Junkies have undeveloped superegos. The inference often plays a role in understanding junkie social acts. What does an ethnographer do with it? First of all, the concepts in the inference point to schemas, but no information is provided on the inferences contained within them or on the conditions under which they might apply. In fact, in its vague present form we have a candidate for a self-validating proposition.

Ethnography requires that schemas be developed in coordination with the analysis of strips. Let's say we use a life history interview with a heroin addict. In analyzing a segment of the interviews, we see an elaborate description. The story is set in a coffeeshop. A woman walks in, sets her purse on a chair, orders some food, and then walks to a vending machine to buy cigarettes. The junkie-narrator comments on her naivete. Then he describes how he simply picked up the purse and walked out the door. He finds $50 inside.

Our analysis shows that we can understand the text with a fairly straightforward means-ends type of schema. Concerns with interpersonal ethics, considerations of the emotional consequences for the victim, and so on, are not required. We decide that the analysis is well served by the "lack of superego" schema. But then we apply it to a new strip contained in the life history where the narrator gives a different description.

In this story, he takes an expensive vase from a friend's house. The story is loaded with expressions of regret—the friend is "good people." She has often helped him out. He "kidded himself" that he would pay her back. But, he explains, he was sick and needed the money. The breakdown caused by this segment motivates the development of a schema about junkie interpersonal morality. But how does the new schema interact with the old one about the lack of superego?

First of all, we have just complicated the superego schema. That is exactly what we want to encourage. One of the strengths of ethnography is that this sort of complication frequently occurs with the propositions characteristic of most social science theory. Unfortunately, such results could lead to a "not my people" critique of psychiatry, or a vacuous "your theory is too simple" response. Instead, we require even more iteration of the schemas against strips, with an eventual schema resolution that shows how the two (and others) interrelate such that certain acts are understood in terms of lack of superego, others in terms of interpersonal morality, and others in terms of conflict between the two.

Now for an example of the second type of theory inference, the type that does not connect directly with strips. We just learned that some junkie acts can be understood in terms of a "no superego" schema and others are better understood in terms of an "interpersonal morality" schema. Why? We have the schemas we need, but now we seek theory inferences that link them up—in the earlier terminology, we want some schema resolution.

Suppose we have a theory of American society that runs something like this: Most junkies come from the slums, barrios, and ghettos of the urban United States. They learn that economic survival will not come from occupational roles available in the larger society; instead, they seek alternatives to survival that rely on the clever manipulation of those persons or institutions that have such resources. Stealing money from someone is nothing personal; it is just an available way to get resources, made more salient by the absence of alternatives. This does not mean that junkies have no principles about who they steal from. They do, and when they steal from such people we expect an account of the extraordinary circumstances that warranted it. On the other hand, when they steal from the usual victims, we expect no such account.

Assume that this theory schema works to solve the immediate problem. At the same time, it sets up new questions that can only be checked out against other interviews, or other ethnographies. For example, not all junkies come from impoverished backgrounds; not all persons from impoverished backgrounds act in ways that the schema suggests; not all who act in ways that the schema suggests are junkies; junkies often steal primarily from other poor people; and so on and so forth. The schema, in short, sets up comparative questions that are the stuff of ethnology.

The use of inferences and schemas from theory presented here fits into the time-honored emic/etic debate in an interesting way. Strips are mostly (but not completely) an accomplishment of the folks, and schema construction is mostly (but not completely) an accomplishment of the ethnographer. We recognize that informant accounts, social theory, creative insight, and many other sources can contribute schematic material. Rather than insisting on a division of ethnographic statements into emic and etic, the language emphasizes their many connections in any ethnography and requires that the connections be made explicit and eventually anchored to the strips that serve as ethnographic data.

4. ETHNOGRAPHIC LANGUAGE AND ETHNOGRAPHIC METHOD

So far the ethnographic language sets no limits on the kinds of resolutions that are acceptable. For example, let's say that at the moment a racist resolution of strips is adequate. "He did that? Oh well, what would you expect from an X," where X can be filled in with the ethnic group of the reader's choice. In other words, given a strip where an X does something that is not coherent given the outsider's schemas, one simply notes that the inability to do so is exactly what characterizes the X as inferior.

Other resolutions, although more subtle, still fail our intuitions about ethnographic adequacy. For example, there are theory schemas that may have something to do with resolving a breakdown, but we want to challenge them. Consider the use of methadone as a street narcotic in the mid-1970s in New York. A policy analyst might say, "Of course they're using methadone; the police cracked down on heroin and the doctors put up hundreds of clinics." A more biochemical type might say, "Of course they use methadone; they suffer from deficits in the production of endogenous opiates." A traditional psychoanalyst might say, "Of course they use methadone; it resolves a pathology which was generated by early childhood encounters with family members." As a final example, an economist might say, "Of course they use methadone; they are social casualties of the changing labor market."

These are simple examples of a policy-oriented, a biological, a psychiatric, and an economic resolution of the shift from heroin to methadone. There is some truth in all of them. At the same time, they are too distant from our ethnographic goal of understanding a variety of informant-controlled strips and too narrow in their coverage. We do not necessarily want to throw them out, but somehow they must fit in with other schemas we construct. An ethnographic language should guide us into ways to talk more explicitly and systematically about why some resolutions are not "ethnographically adequate." To begin to do so, we turn to the first type of ethnographic evidence—the use of strips to mandate breakdowns.

Anticoherence

Ethnographers frequently try to force breakdowns to occur. Even when they think they understand some strip, they work to bring about a problem in understanding. One way to think about mandating breakdowns is by way of a general attitude of anticoherence. In this attitude, understanding is suspect; you self-consciously try to show that "what I think is going on probably isn't." Anticoherence is not supposed to encourage solipsism or borderline psychosis, nor is it a mechanical method that produces the same results on repeated application. It simply represents a stance toward strips that helps narrow the range of acceptable resolutions.

Getting a grip on anticoherence (if you'll excuse the paradox) requires a better sense of how coherence relates to strips. Whatever level they are on, whoever controls them, and whether or not they are recorded, strips are the arena within which breakdowns can be forced. What does it mean for the coherence of a strip to be called into question? In our collaboration over the last couple of years, Jerry Hobbs and I have tried to specify one version of coherence in the analysis of an extensive life history (Agar and Hobbs, 1985). For the present, I would like to modify and extend some of this work as it generally applies to strips.

In order to talk about parts of a strip, Hobbs and I used the word "segment." Notice that "strip" and "segment" can adjust relative to each other to take in broader or narrower scope. In our work, we usually take a single one- to two-hour interview as a strip, and then divide it into topically continuous segments. At a higher level, one could take the entire life history as the strip, and specify each interview as a segment. Or at a lower level, one could take part of a single interview as the strip, and each utterance within it as a segment. Similar variations would apply to observations as well as interviews.

In an anticoherent attitude three different kinds of questions can be asked. The first emphasizes the relationships between two adjacent segments. This type, called *segmental coherence*, raises the question, What inferences do I need to make to understand why segment X and segment Y follow each other? The second kind, called *strip coherence*, leads us to ask, "What inferences do I need to make to understand how segment X is related to the other schemas I have constructed to understand the strip as a whole?"

The third kind, called *thematic coherence*, requires us to ask, "Of the inferences I make to understand segment X, are any of them related to understandings of other segments in other strips?"

To demonstrate the application of the questions, return once more to the charcoal theory. Placing the charcoal in the lunch was segmentally coherent with the preceding act of putting the food in the cloth and the following act of wrapping it shut. It was also strip-coherent with the cook's sense of spirits and his plan to protect me. If I had known enough, it would also have been strip-coherent with my plan to avoid spirit attacks. The act was thematically coherent with the recurrently important conventions about spirits, as well as the cook's goal of keeping a protective eye on me. In this example, the three different questions lead to three coherent views.

On the other hand, a segment may be coherent under one kind of question but not under others. A group member might be telling a story, be reminded of something in the course of telling it, start to get into what Hobbs and I call an "associative slide," but then realize what is going on and return to the story. For example, I might tell you "I was typing this book, and it reminded me once of when I was typing and a cockroach crawled out of the typewriter. I didn't know whether to—but that's getting away from the point." Slides like this are perfect examples of utterance segments that, although coherent from one to another, are strip-incoherent and look like they won't lead to any interesting themes.

Consider another example. I walk downstairs from my apartment and put some clothes in the dryer. Then I walk to the corner coffee shop and have a conversation about hermeneutics. What do these two segments have to do with each other? Only a stretch of the imagination would produce a segmentally coherent relationship, except in the trivial sense that one act followed the other in time and space. Similarly, an effort to establish thematic coherence would be difficult. Except for the observation that both dryers and hermeneutics involve circular motion and hot air, themes would elude us. On the other hand, we might show that each segment is *individually* strip-coherent. The first was part of a plan to do some household chores; the second occurred because of a scheduled conversation. The two segments are strip-coherent, but with reference to different plans.

The three questions suggest ways of mandating breakdowns in understanding. As the examples indicate, they do not guarantee coherence, as a segment may turn out under repeated attempts not to lend itself to coherent understanding. But in that case, an ethnographer can show how it is that a segment or strip is coherent in one way but not in another.

We now have a way to talk about an anticoherent attitude. One can mandate breakdowns in at least three ways for any strip:

(1) What inferences do I have to make to understand why segment n – 1, segment n, and segment n + 1 in the strip follow each other?
(2) What inferences do I have to make to understand how segment n in the strip is connected to the other schemas in terms of which that strip is understood?
(3) How are the inferences I make to understand segment n in the strip related to inferences I make to understand segments in other strips?

We can use the coherence questions separately for each level of a strip. For example, suppose I did an informal ethnographic interview about the charcoal incident. I could ask questions at level 2 to understand in terms of the situation itself. But I could also ask the questions at level 1 to analyze it as conversation between ethnographer and informant.

Forced attention to the details of a strip requires us to alter schemas by showing how inferences have to be added, deleted, or rearranged to demonstrate the strip's coherence. Alternately, a strip may be coherent in some ways but not in others, but then we must show the schemas in terms of which that claim is made. The use of the coherence questions gives us one version of evidence. We have adequate evidence, in part, when the questions no longer cause any breakdowns.

This argument has its parallels elsewhere. Labov and Fanshel (1977), in their analysis of a segment of a psychiatric interview, point out that most discussions of such interviews offer summaries and general statements unanchored in actual examples of interview sessions. A similar critique is made for sociology by Cicourel (1974, 1975) because many in that field analyze data consisting of records or interview responses. He argues that such data are an abstraction from strips, and that without a sense of the "interpretive procedures" used by the analyst it is impossible to understand what the abstraction means. Finally, it is a classic criticism of ethnographic reports that they present general conclusions with a few supporting anecdotes. An anecdote taken as a strip is a valuable ethnographic resource, but it must be balanced with other kinds of strips and analyzed in some detail.

The emphasis on careful attention to strips via the coherence questions fits in with my experience of how ethnography works. In addition to breakdowns that come up serendipitously, others can be mandated by applying the questions to strips in an anticoherent attitude. This limits the possible resolutions that are ethnographically adequate. Consider an oversimplified example—an ethnographer wants to understand strips primarily in terms of power differences among the different participants. An application of this general schema to strips in terms of coherence questions will produce several breakdowns. If an analyst is going to maintain this position, he or she must do one of two things:

(1) construct inferences that connect the strip segments coherently with the schema, or
(2) show why it is that the schema does not apply to segments of the strip.

In either case, the questions block the simple, direct use of high-level schemas and force the development of more detailed ones, and that is exactly what we want ethnography to do.

On the other hand, nothing prevents us from creatively imagining all kinds of bizarre inferential links that answer the coherence questions quite readily. We might consider some of these unworthy of attention because their byzantine nature so strains our credibility. On the other hand, there may also be different schemas that do equally well at resolving breakdowns—in fact, there may be several.

Some constraints are set by the thematic coherence question. Schemas assembled to enable understanding of a single strip may turn out to be ad hoc constructions that help us with that strip and little else. As one works through different resolutions, the research process pushes the thematic schemas to the foreground. The preference is for schemas that routinely apply to a wide range of strips rather than for the idiosyncratic schema that works only in one or two cases.

One reason that the notion of schema was developed was to show how expectations work in understanding. Once a schema is called into play, it suggests expectations about what else might be going on. This characteristic leads to a second kind of methodological implication of the language, one that ties in with thematic coherence—the display of comprehension.

Comprehension Displays

An anticoherent attitude challenges our understanding of strips and improves the chances that new schemas will be required. But we also want to test the value of the new schemas by trying them out against additional strips to see if they help us *comprehend* them as well. Comprehension can be displayed in a variety of ways. One classic test that some ethnographers aspire to is "if you think you understand the X, then you should be able to act like the X." This goal is represented, for example, in Goodenough's (1957) definition of "culture" as the knowledge necessary to behave appropriately. Sometimes this strategy may work quite well, but there are some problems with it. An ethnographer's behavior may not always be as "correctable" as it should be for this kind of validation to work.

In the midst of a bit of group life, with many members present, politeness may prohibit informants from commenting on mistakes, resulting in an ethnographer feeling successful when in fact the group thinks he or she is behaving improperly. Besides, an apparent mistake in the ethnographer's behavior may be due to a variety of things besides lack of understanding. As a newcomer struggling with his or her own tradition as well as another tradition, the ethnographer may comprehend acts while muffing the enactment of a situation. The ability to "act like a native" may be important, even critical from some points of view. But it should not be the only, or even the privileged, type of evidence for comprehension.

Fortunately, other tests are possible. Schemas can be validated in at least two other ways. First, an ethnographer can check his or her ability to apply a schema correctly during the flow of daily life. One way to test this is simply to name the schema that renders the strip sensible and then see if informants agree or disagree.

Naming may require anything from a lexeme to a sequence of utterances—any chunk of language that describes the schema that plausibly applies. Ethnographers must be able to (1) characterize the schema in informant language and (2) have some sense of when a schema applies to strips (either through invariant characteristics of the schema or through inferences contained within it) such that (3) they can discuss with informants "what is going on" to test their comprehension.

The same test works with the higher-level schemas discussed earlier, although the application is less direct. What if we have a sense that much of what is going on has to do with powerlessness, for example? For now, we just note that such higher-level schemas, while perhaps not easily represented in informant language, must connect through inferences to schemas that do allow for a coherent discussion.

Other tests of comprehension can be more subtle. A schema allows an ethnographer to make numerous inferences. Given a sense of which schemas apply, any inference can serve as a source of questions for an ethnographer to ask or to check through observation. Once you figure out you are at a wedding in a South Indian village, your new schemas tell you that there should be a drummer. You look around and there he is. Or perhaps you look around and one is not there; the failed inference leads you to ask questions. Maybe the group members are wondering too; maybe you just missed him; maybe you've got the wrong schema; or maybe you've just brought about a derivative breakdown and now return to the coherence questions discussed earlier.

So far, these examples of the display of comprehension through application or inference have emphasized informant-controlled level-1 strips. If the schema can be checked by observation and naming, the test will hardly interrupt the flow of action. As soon as an ethnographer begins to ask more elaborate questions, however, the strip shifts to level 2 with more ethnographer control.

The amount of control can vary a good bit. Ethnographers may just ask a brief informal question of an informant standing nearby during an event. Or they may initiate a tape-recorded interview where several applications and inferences can be talked about. Or they may design a specific list of questions to be administered to a controlled sample—questions that are based on and designed to test comprehension of some key schemas. At this point ethnographers can use the received view, hypothesis-testing models of social research. But the problem for ethnography is that much evidence for comprehension is accumulated in unscheduled, informal ways. Such evidence is powerful and appropriate to the goals of the research but is difficult to document. The methodological problem is to figure out when, in what way, and how much to do this documentation. It is a difficult problem, but not an impossible one.

However the ethnographer chooses to check comprehension, informants may respond in a variety of ways. At one extreme, they might indicate that the ethnographer is not making sense—a "what are you talking about" response. At the other, they might indicate that the ethnographer has hit a key inference—a "you've got it" response. But in-between are a number of other possibilities. A near miss might be indicated by a "sort of" response. A complex piece of social action might get a "that's one way of looking at it." A strip where several things are going on at the same time might get a correction to a schema different from the one the ethnographer is using. An act that is in fact an area where group members often disagree might elicit a quick but elaborate and coherent counterargument showing why the schema is completely wrong. Finally, the inferences of some schemas may work for the ethnographer although their application is denied.

5. THE LANGUAGE IN USE: TWO EXAMPLES

The ethnographic language outlined here characterizes only a part of what an ethnographer does. That part—perhaps the most critical when it comes to the public display of knowledge—occurs when the ethnographer detaches and analyzes, when he or she works to reason from some data to some pattern. But nothing in the language *directly* represents the human relationships or the sensitive face-to-face understanding without which ethnographic reports sound flat. The human dimensions of the experience will be *indirectly* reflected in many ways, however. There are several reasons for this:

(1) Most ethnographers hold to a general axiom that the longer and better one gets to know the folks, the richer and more complex will be the understandings that result.
(2) "Rapport" is a codeword for the quality of the relationships the ethnographer has with the folks. In terms of the language developed here, without rapport people wouldn't let you into their world or talk to you about it—no informant-controlled strips and no informant help in schema construction. Similarly for "participant observation," a schizophrenogenic concept if ever there was one. From the viewpoint of the ethnographic language outlined in this book, participant observation is neither

a method nor a type of data; instead, it describes the situation that allows high-quality breakdowns and resolutions to happen at all.

(3) Many things are learned during the research that are not converted into strips for analysis. Some things are too private, from either the ethnographer's or the group's point of view. Some things are too difficult to represent, such as the superficially insignificant event that for unknown reasons triggers a fundamental ethnographic "aha." Some things are too involving—you're too busy doing them to worry about a record. It doesn't matter. The world is full of actions that can be bounded, lifted out, and contemplated as strips. But the other things you learn show up indirectly in the schemas you construct to understand those experiences that do go into the pool of data.

Ethnography is not just a process of resolving schemas. If it were, I doubt many of us would do it. Human understanding works in mysterious ways, and fieldwork experiences have meanings that go far beyond one's "official" researcher role. But part of what ethnographers do *is* detached, analytic, and systematic, and it is this part that is most at stake when they draw back from the personal nature of the experience and concern themselves with a public presentation of a coherent view of a "humanscape" that is new to the eyes of the reader. That is what an ethnographic language is for.

Example 1:
The Life History of an Addict

Given that the language is limited in scope, focusing on the analytic part of ethnographic work, is it useful? So far I have used it twice. Both uses are published elsewhere, but I would like to sketch them here. The first project, one that in fact contributed to the development of the language outlined in this book, was the analysis of a heroin addict's life history that I have referred to earlier, done in collaboration with Jerry Hobbs (Agar and Hobbs, 1985).

Here's a sample of a passage from Jack's interview, transcribed for readability rather than linguistic accuracy:

> Meanwhile Frenchy's called me to come over and sit at the table with him. So you know, I looked at these two kids, and I-I sat down at the table, and I was just in no mood to listen to a lot of bullshit. So I turned to the kids, I said, "Hey, look you guys, why don't you just soft peddle it?" I said, "I don't know what your story is and I care less, but you're making a general display of yourself. This place is loaded with rats. It's only going to be a matter of time until a cop comes in and busts the whole table." I told Frenchy, I said, "Frenchy, what the fuck is the matter with you?" you know. I says, "Why don't you tell these dudes to shut up?" "But Jack, they've got blah blah blah," you know. "And I want to get this stuff." I said, "Well look," I said, "You guys may not care if you go to jail, but I do." I said, "I spend 75 percent of my time trying to stay out of jail, and I don't want anybody to come up here and bother us."

In the interview Jack is telling the story of how he learned to be a burglar. In this segment, he talks about how he first met "Johnny" (one of the kids at the table), who it turns out later is the one who teaches him burglary. In the full analysis, Hobbs and I apply the coherence questions at several different levels for this particular level-2, tape-recorded segment. For now I want to focus on the schema we grew out of this passage and the thematic work we did with it.

The kids (we learned in a preceding segment of the interview) are waving stolen goods around to impress Frenchy, the "fence," or buyer of stolen goods. Jack is also looking for Frenchy because he wants to sell him some gloves and a watch that he stole from a guy's luggage in a train station. In the segment, Jack lays out a tentative schema detailing the relationships among competence as a street hustler, attracting attention, and avoiding arrest. The kids are naive or stupid, waving around stolen goods in a public place in a way that might get them all busted.

After using the text and the coherence questions to develop the schema, we asked the thematic coherence question: How did the schema apply to other segments? We first drew on our knowledge of junkie life and noted that any mention of an illegal act (hustle) should automatically make the schema relevant. We went through the rest of the interview and lifted out portions of text where hustles were mentioned. We identified 15. In some cases they were parts of segments, in some they were an entire segment, and in one case a portion was three segments long.

For convenience, I'll refer to the portions by the numbers we assigned them in the original analysis, 1 through 15. When the original tentative schema is applied to the new strips, two major enrichments result. First, we learn the intricate relationship between competence at a particular hustle and the ability to avoid the attention that might lead to arrest. Second, we learn some of the details of what goes into competence for a house burgler. Let me deal with the first enrichment first.

Portions 2 and 3 mention two hustles—buying heroin and breaking into cars—that are routine for Jack at the time of the story. In fact, he explicitly mentions his familiarity with breaking into cars in 3. These hustles are practiced skills. The arrest schema is noteworthy due to its absence, supporting our initial impressions that the arrest schema is less salient when one knows what one is doing. For example, here's part of portion 3:

> We got off the ferry and we started to walk. Now I had already been broken into, you know, cracking cars and taking stuff out of the back seat and stuff like that, luggage and radios and stuff of that sort. So I thought well the least I can do is you know keep my eye open. If I see a good take, why this'll sort of pay up a little bit. So I'm kind of casing cars, but he has no-no time for this.

The relationship of schema to segment is further supported when we consider the different accounts Jack gives of burglaries. In 4 and 5, where Jack reports the first burglary that Johnny (his teacher) led him into, he describes his anxiety, explaining it by his lack of knowledge of how to do a burglary and his fear of attracting attention. For example, "I was-I was-I was so nervous that I didn't know what I was doing, you know." As in the original segment, there is a relationship between competence and risk of arrest. "Every step I took I expected to hear the siren." The schema that we grew out of the first segment generalizes to cover several more.

As the interview progresses, Jack gives examples of other burglaries. The tone changes dramatically from the first description. In 6, although he again mentions his fear of attracting attention, we also see an account of some of the details of a burglary schema (to be discussed shortly). In 9 another burglary story shows additional competence in the details, and ends with a matter-of-fact story of how Johnny and Jack left through one door while the occupants came in another. In contrast to the first burglary, anxiety about arrest is notable because of its absence. In 15—yet another burglary story—details are again described, but the story ends with Jack and Johnny running out through the returning occupants. In the first burglary description this would have led Jack to panic; now it's the climax to a "funny" story.

The comments on scoring heroin and breaking into cars, together with the decline in anxiety about arrest in the different descriptions of burglaries, support the original schema. Now let's focus more on the issue of attracting attention. In 6, 8 and 15 Jack comments on how much less attentive people are than he expected. In 7 he talks about how proper use of a car helps avoid attention. "I preferred to have her drive, because he was excitable, and he would gun a car away from the place, and she would pull away with just you know just as a calm as a cucumber, and you know it would attract no attention." In 8 he comments on the importance of dressing so that one blends in with the ambient social world. "But we carried ourselves well. We were always immaculately clean, and we didn't look you know—we never wore baggy trousers. We didn't dress in typical diddy bop fashion." We learn that Jack was overconcerned, and that at any rate there are things you can do to further reduce the attention you attract.

Next we learn an interesting link between attracting attention and the details of the burglary schemas as Jack reports them. In several places Jack lays out some of those details. In 6 he notes that one picks a house because it is isolated (on top of a hill, surrounded by trees). One also works at certain times, when people are unlikely to return home and one can expect neighbors to be busy. Finally, one breaks in using quiet techniques. In 5 and 9 we see that one must learn what the best things are to take—easily portable, high-value items. In 12 the importance of a good partner is emphasized, somebody who will keep an eye out for the police. And we also learn of the importance of a second exit to use in an emergency. In 15 another burglary is described. The importance of house selection is again mentioned (isolated, surrounded by trees, vacant lot next door), as is proper appearance and a good car. As a woman now works with them, she goes to the house first to check if anybody is home. Again the importance of knowing what to take and the two exits comes up.

The interesting issue at the moment is the number of details that in fact specify how to avoid attention or how to set up strategies to deal with it if one is noticed. This further supports our original impressions about the link between arrest and hustling competence. Part of Jack's growing competence as a burglar is in fact knowledge about avoiding attention.

The schema is related in different ways to other portions as well. For example, in 10 fences are evaluated negatively just because they profit from the hustles of others without the risk of arrest that comes with stealing the goods. In 1 the use of a room at the YMCA by two people when only one paid motivates a "then/now" comment as Jack explains that in those days this involved no risk of getting caught.

Even more interesting is the elaborate (three-segment) account of Jack's eventual arrest (14). The story justifies the core concern represented in the schema because it describes in detail the difficulties that ensue on arrest and conviction. Second, the story shows one problem that the schema does not represent—Johnny is busted after his return to Detroit, and under police pressure he tells the whole story. This leads to Jack's arrest when he is picked up in connection with another hustle in which, in fact, he was not involved. Plea bargaining with arrested suspects in return for information is a well-known police strategy, and the story in this interview shows how it relates to the schema.

By taking the schema through this multiple-strip resolution process, we validate and enrich it. We wind up with a simple core to the schema—hustles enable arrest enables conviction and incarceration. However, arrest has as a precondition information and/or evidence of some sort, obtained either by the police directly, through an informer, or from the victim. So we can schema-resolve and say that a major problem for the hustler is to block the precondition by preventing information from reaching the police, or, as we have been saying here, by avoiding attention. In the interview we learn that failure to do so is occasion for comment, argument, and lecture. From a street point of view, one who violates the expectations represented in the schema is not competent.

We also generalize the schema and set up some potential comprehension displays to guide our next encounters with discussions of hustles. The schema points to some important details that should be found in the schema for any hustle. Not only does one minimize attention by knowing the hustle and carrying it out smoothly. In addition, a schema for any hustle will contain within it knowledge about ways to avoid attention that are specific to the activities it represents. Further, we expect that the schemas will also contain strategies to use should the hustle in fact attract the attention of people who may serve as information conduits to the police.

The example of Jack's interview illustrates the language in action, but the example is a narrow one. Does the language apply at a more general level of description of an ethnographic study?

Yes, it does. But rather than use another drug example, let me shift the scene to a recent ethnography I did with owner-operators, individuals who own and operate their own tractor-trailers.

Example 2: Independent Trucking

A few years ago I began a study of the working world of independent truckers. My first contact with them, at a trade organization meeting in Baltimore in mid-1981, led to an invitation to explain my work and what I wanted to do. After I had done so, a general discussion among the members expressed a favorable attitude toward my proposed study. The reason? The popular image of the independent trucker—*Convoy, BJ and the Bear, Smokey and the Bandit*—was ridiculous from their point of view. At that time I did not understand why they talked so much about the popular image in such a negative way. I had just experienced an occasioned breakdown that would become core by the end of my research.

In the trucking study all kinds of strips were used as data. Taped and transcribed career history interviews were one type. The notes from three cross-country and several regional trips were another, not to mention notes from the monthly meetings of the Baltimore organization. I followed trucking industry trade publications and attended hearings in various Washington, D.C., settings. Archival work in the Interstate Commerce Commission and the Department of Transportation yielded still more material. And there were hundreds of conversations with independents and family members, as well as other people involved in the trucking industry, at meetings, truck stops, and social gatherings. The usual ethnographic problem: more potential strips than you know what to do with.

In order to organize the analysis, some strips were defined as the "corpus" for which I had to account, while others were left for more casual use. Because of my bias toward linguistic data, I put the career history interviews in the corpus. Each interview was marked off into segments just as Hobbs and I had done with the life history. But then, instead of pushing into the segments for an utterance-by-utterance view of things, segments were simply coded for broad areas of topical content in the usual, old-fashioned ethnographic way. Groups of topically related segments became the strips with which to build and validate schemas.

Unlike the life history work, however, schemas were built in prose instead of formalisms. My general strategy was to take an example segment and then write informally about the new knowledge needed by the nontrucker to understand it. This new knowledge came from a variety of other strips, as well as from ethnographic insight, whatever that is. A particular schema might draw from a bit of economics, some facts about the organization of the trucking industry, something about the speaker, and an observation from a trip. For example, here's a brief segment, edited for readability:

> There's an outfit that called me Friday that I was thinking about going to work for. I understand they're pretty decent. Now they were a bad outfit, but apparently they found the error of their ways. Take Mark Transport that I worked for, for instance. When they started cutting their rates and they lost their drivers they probably had about 20 guys working for them at one time when I worked down there. Then as the work started tapering off they drifted off into other directions. Now if Mark runs an ad in the Baltimore paper for an owner-operator and a guy calls in, as soon as you say it's Mark Transport they'll hang up on you.

To understand this passage, you need to know a variety of things. Among them are the following: (1) Most truckers who own and operate their own tractor lease on as independent contractors to trucking companies to get freight. (2) Companies set the rates—the price charged for hauling the freight. (3) During my study deregulation of trucking began and the United States experienced an economic recession. The result was declining rates. (4) Many independents are paid on a percentage of the revenue for a load of freight. When rates are cut, they—not the trucking company—absorb most of the loss. (5) On a trip I took, I saw the power of the recession in drying up the availability of freight to haul. (6) This particular interviewee is shopping around for a new trucking company, so there are many comparisons of different companies in his interview.

The analysis works by taking that kind of knowledge and transforming it into readable prose. The monograph presents the analysis by interspersing segments with prose schemas. As it moves along, a particular resolution can presuppose the resolutions already accomplished, so later schemas get either simpler or more fine-grained—simpler because the new knowledge has already been presented, or more fine-grained because, based on that new knowledge, even greater schematic detail is possible. If the organization of the material works as it should, readers learn as they go how the pieces fit together—an informal version of the more technical concept of schema resolution introduced earlier.

The segments in the interviews deal with a number of topics—relationships with trucking companies to whom the independents' were leased, with state and federal regulatory bodies, with shippers (those who provide the freight) and customers (those who receive it), and with the mechanics who rescue you on the road. As the different schemas were built to make sense of all this, schema resolution suggested questions about what those different schemas had to do with each other. One answer—which became overwhelming as the analysis moved along—was that most of the specific resolutions highlighted a theme of *dependence*. Interviewees described themselves as caught up in a world where they had to depend on others and where, as the powerless one in the relationship, they were usually taken advantage of.

The next problem in the analysis was to bring in resolutions of other strips and "schema-resolve" them with the dependency theme. One group of strips came from observations on trips—strips more akin to traditional "field notes" than to interview transcripts. The resolution of the notes with the transcripts yielded an interesting result—the interview-based schemas were *true* as accounts of dependency, but *overstated* as reports of disastrous outcomes resulting from that dependency. For example, interviews contained several stories about how shippers and customers routinely held you up when you went to load or unload. But on the trips I took severe delays were rare. Why the discrepancy?

With that breakdown in mind, another set of strips was brought into play—the texts of popular novels that presented the idealized image of independent truckers. By schema-resolving them with the previous material, a truth emerged: The popular image, representing the old American frontier myth, left out almost all the details of the working world that the interviews contained. So, this became one conclusion of the study: When independent truckers talk about their work, the theme of dependency is overwhelming. Observations on actual trips indicate that disastrous outcomes do not occur as often as the interviews suggest. But the disasters do highlight the major differences between the image in the popular literature and the nature of their working world. Independent truckers, in brief, are caught in a sociocultural squeeze play. They are used to personify a traditional American cultural myth while experiencing work-based social relationships that contradict it. No wonder they complained so much about *Convoy* at that first meeting.

In a couple of cases, the difference between image and reality was a topic in the interviews, like in this taped exchange between two independents:

> DAVE: You know that's just about like—here back awhile I was reading in *Overdrive*. This driver was talking to this TV fellow about, you know, they got like *BJ and the Bear*.
>
> STEVE: Hasn't helped the industry any.
>
> DAVE: Let's see, what was that other one that was on there that had . . .

STEVE: Sonny and Will

DAVE: Yeah.

STEVE: *Moving On.*

DAVE: *Moving On* and all them. He says, "You know, you watch one of these shows and you get this conception about what it's like to go truck driving that's totally unreal. Why don't you put something on there about the actual events that a trucker goes through in a day?" And so they went out and they'd go, you know. He's going around this and that and the other. And they get it all done and they ask him what he thinks of it. And he says, "Yeah, that's pretty good." He says, "You going to run it?" "No."

STEVE: Nobody'd ever believe it.

DAVE: Says, "Why not?" "Nobody'd ever believe it."

With that I had returned to the occasioned breakdown that began the study. The ethnographic language proposed here helped conceptualize the study and guided the analysis from initial contact with the group through preparation of the final monograph. Even though this study was quite different from the life history work, the language was useful in both (although I'm hardly an impartial judge).

The Examples Compared

The analysis of the life history pretty much followed the language as outlined in this book. Hobbs and I focused on a strip, applied coherence questions to mandate breakdowns, and built a schema to resolve them. The schema was an explicit formal propositional representation. Then we looked at other segments of the interview to do multiple-strip resolution, developing the thematic nature of the schema we had built up along the way. The research was "ethnographic," but it obviously had some unique twists:

(1) To say that the range of coverage of strips was limited would be generous. Most of the analysis was based on two interviews.

(2) The analysis of such limited material came at the end of 12 years of on-again, off-again work with heroin addicts. We were short on data but long on material for schema construction.
(3) The article that resulted more or less replicates the actual process of analysis; it is presented in an academic style that also includes some artificial intelligence formalisms.

The second study, done *after* the development of the language used here, is an investigation of the working world of independent truckers. The study began with an occasioned breakdown—a trucker discussion of the distortions in the popular depiction of their role—and that breakdown became core. Some strips were defined as the focus—transcripts of career history interviews. But the study involved other kinds of experiences that often go into an ethnography—direct participation in their world, informal conversations, and so on. The ethnographic language was useful in thinking about and organizing the research during its conduct and when analyzing and writing later. As I was aiming the book at a general audience, the results look different from the work that Hobbs and I did:

(1) Strips were of all the types defined earlier, varying in control, record, and level. To organize the book, I defined excerpts from the level-2, informant-controlled, tape-recorded interviews as the core strips to motivate and validate schemas. Material from other strips was brought in more casually in a supplementary role.
(2) Schemas were presented in ordinary prose. The usual format was to present an excerpt from an interview (strip) together with some prose that gave the new knowledge required to understand it coherently (schema).
(3) The monograph has a more distant relationship to the process of analysis when compared to the article Hobbs and I wrote. It is more oriented to the conclusions of the process rather than to its history.

The difference here is primarily one of audience. The article with Hobbs was directed at a technical audience with a "here's the details of how this works" message. The book was aimed at a general audience with a "here's some interesting things about the working world of independent truckers" message. The style of reporting changes with the intended audience. The difference is not surprising. If I tell engineers about a building I'm working on, they might ask about the scaffolding; if I talk to the people who are about to move in, they'll wonder about the floorplan; if tourists happen by, they might want to talk generally about its history. The language here was useful, and it's also helpful in talking to professional colleagues about the details of the work. But a more general audience could care less about the scaffolding; they want to know what the building looks like. An ethnographic language, in short, does *not* prescribe the form of an ethnographic report.

6. CONCLUSION

The ethnographic language proposed in this book is an alternative to the received view of science—the view tenaciously held by many American social scientists—that centers around the testing of hypotheses. Some responses to the earlier articles on which this book is based point out that what I describe as *different* from the received view is actually what scientists do (Kirk and Miller, 1983). I have no quarrel with that; in fact, if you read some of the popular versions of what the theoretical physicists are up to it makes the ethnographic language set out here look positivistic by comparison.

But if you listen to discussions about social research, whether the speakers are professionals or laypersons, you hear the old bells tolling—"What's your hypothesis?" "What's the independent variable?" "How can you generalize with such a small sample?" "How do you measure that?" "Did you get an intercoder reliability figure?" "Who did you use for a control group?" Those are important questions for some research, including, oftentimes, parts of an ethnographic study. But they simply miss the point of much of what goes into ethnography.

Criticizing the received view does not mean that there is no systematic alternative. As the philosopher Gadamer writes in the preface to the second edition of *Truth and Method*, after his ideas had been used by some to reject science,

> If there is any practical consequence of the present investigation, it certainly has nothing to do with an unscientific "commitment"; instead, it is concerned with the "scientific" integrity of acknowledging the commitment involved in all understanding [1975: xvi].

The ethnographic language proposed in this book is an effort to find a sensible way to talk about an ethnographer's work that is helpful to those who do it, a way that preserves the key elements of publicly reasoning from data to conclusion in a style that tries to prove oneself wrong as often as possible. Hypothesis testing it isn't, although it can include it when appropriate. Systematic it is, although the ethnographer becomes part of a study that grows unexpected patterns that increase in complexity with his or her experience, patterns through which one group of folks can make sense of what some others are doing.

In this book the emphasis has been on the language as a way for ethnographers to talk about the analysis of the folks. Others, who read the earlier articles on which this book is based, suggest that it describes more than just that. For example, McElroy and Jezewski (1984) applied the language to interaction between doctor and patient in a pediatric clinic. They found that the interactants themselves were also experiencing and resolving breakdowns, so they used the language as a model for what the folk were doing with each other's expressions as well as a model for what the ethnographer was doing with the expressions produced by the folk. Whitehead (1984) used the language to talk about resolving breakdowns during his fieldwork in a West

Indian community, but he emphasized the analysis of change in his *own* tradition. His resolution of an analytic problem led him to see his tradition differently, demonstrating the "dialogic" nature of interpretation in a way that my presentation neglects.

Their work also suggests that the language may be more than just an ethnographic one. Considering that many of the ideas behind the book are related to ideas in several different fields, it's no surprise that the language sometimes resembles theories from those fields as well. Pleasant as the broader range of application and the many potential links to other fields may be to contemplate, the goal of this book is satisfied. That goal is to propose an alternative to the received view, an alternative that liberates ethnography from a language within which it cannot succeed and places it inside a language that represents its complexity as a research style and the sophistication required for its successful practice.

At the same time, the language shifts our sense of some fundamental concepts in cultural anthropology. If ethnography describes a culture, then "culture" becomes a name for some bridges that link up different traditions. We do not have to claim "psychological reality" for our descriptions, as we are after an understanding of public expressions rather than a model of how the folks produced them. "Validity" and "reliability" become complex indeed (see Kirk and Miller, 1985). Although not all resolutions are acceptable, several different ones will be, depending on traditions that go into the encounter—strips chosen for analysis, granularity of application of the coherence questions, sources of inferences and schemas, and all the other places where choices get made. If there is a change in the language by which anthropologist-ethnographers characterize the fundamental stuff out of which the field is built, the higher-level concepts that characterize that field will change also.

I hope the ethnographic language proposed here will contribute to and encourage others in reflecting on and articulating the analytic part of the ethnographic research style. Most of the pieces used in this proposed language are borrowed, sometimes without adequate respect for or sophistication in the rich scholarly traditions from which they were taken. At worst, the proposed language can serve as a useful mistake. But with any luck the result is a useful arrangement.

REFERENCES

AGAR, M. (forthcoming) Independents Declared. Washington, DC: Smithsonian Institution Press.

———(1980) The Professional Stranger. New York: Academic Press.

———(1977) "Going through the changes: methadone in New York." Human Organization 36: 291-295.

———and J. HOBBS (1985) "Growing schemas out of interviews," in J. Dougherty (ed.) Directions in Cognitive Anthropology. Urbana: University of Illinois Press.

BARRETT, S. R. (1976) "The use of models in anthropological fieldwork." Journal of Anthropological Research 32: 161-181.

BECKER, A. L. (1982) "On Emerson on language," in D. Tannen (ed.) Analyzing Discourse: Text and Talk. Washington, DC: Georgetown University Press.

BECKER, H. (1970) "Field work evidence," in Sociological Work: Method and Substance. New Brunswick, NJ: Transaction Books.

BRUCE, B. (1980) "Analysis of interacting plans as a guide to the understanding of story structure." Poetics 9: 295-311.

———(1979) A Societal Interaction Model of Reading (BBN Report 4328). Cambridge: Bolt, Beranek & Newman.

CICOUREL, A. (1975) Theory and Method in the Study of Argentine Fertility. New York: John Wiley.

———(1974) "Interpretive procedures and normative rules in the negotiation of status and role," in Cognitive Sociology. New York: Free Press.

CLARK, H. H. (1975) "Bridging," in P. N. Johnson-Laird and P. C. Wason (eds.) Thinking: Readings in Cognitive Science. Cambridge: Cambridge University Press.

COLBY, B. N. and L. COLBY (1981) The Daykeeper. Cambridge: Harvard University Press.

COLBY, B. N. et al. (1981) "Toward a convergence of cognitive and symbolic anthropology." American Ethnologist 8: 422-450.

COLLINGWOOD, R. G. (1978) An Autobiography. Oxford: Oxford University Press.

COLLINS, A. (1978) "Fragments of a theory of human plausible reasoning," in Theoretical Issues in Natural Language (Vol. 2). New York: Association for Computing Memory.

———et al. (1975) "Reasoning from incomplete knowledge," in D. G. Bobrow and A. Collins (eds.) Representation and Understanding. New York: Academic Press.

DEVEREUX, G. (1967) From Anxiety to Method in the Behavioral Sciences. The Hague: Mouton.

FOSTER, G. M., T. SCUDDER, E. COLSON, and R. V. KEMPER (1978) Long-Term Field Research in Social Anthropology. New York: Academic Press.

FRAKE, C. O. (1981) Language and Cultural Description. Stanford: Stanford University Press.

FREEMAN, D. (1983) Margaret Mead and Samoa: The Making and Unmaking of an Anthropological Myth. Cambridge: Harvard University Press.

GADAMER, H. G. (1975) Truth and Method. New York: Continuum.

GARFINKEL, H. (1967) Studies in Ethnomethodology. Englewood Cliffs, NJ: Prentice-Hall.

GEERTZ, C. (1976) "From the native's point of view: on the nature of anthropological understanding," in K. H. Basso and H. A. Selby (eds.) Meaning in Anthropology. Albuquerque: University of New Mexico Press.

———(1973) The Interpretation of Cultures. New York: Basic Books.

GIDDENS, A. (1976) New Rules of Sociological Method. New York: Basic Books.

GLASER, B. and A. STRAUSS (1967) The Discovery of Grounded Theory. Hawthorne, NY: Aldine.

GOFFMAN, E. (1974) Frame Analysis. New York: Harper & Row.

GOODENOUGH, W. (1957) "Cultural anthropology and linguistics." Georgetown University Series on Language and Linguistics 9: 67-173.

GOULD, H. A. (1975) "Two decades of fieldwork in India—some reflections," in A. Beteille and T. N. Madan (eds.) Encounter and Experience: Personal Accounts of Fieldwork. Delhi: Vikas.

GROSZ, B. J. (1978) "Focusing in dialog," in Theoretical Issues in Natural Language (Vol. 2). New York: Association for Computing Memory.

HIRSCH, E. D. (1976) The Aims of Interpretation. Chicago: University of Chicago Press.

HOBBS, J . R. (1978) Why is Discourse Coherent? (SRI Technical Note 176). Menlo Park, CA: SRI International.

HUTCHINS, E. (1980) Culture and Inference. Cambridge: Harvard University Press.

KEMPTON, W. (1978) "Category grading and taxonomic relations." American Ethnologist 5: 44-65.

KIRK, J. and M. L. MILLER (1985) Reliability and Validity in Qualitative Research. Beverly Hills, CA: Sage.

———(1983) "Ethnography, hermeneutics and science: a response to Agar." (unpublished)

LABOV, W. and D. FANSHEL (1977) Therapeutic Discourse: Psychotherapy as Conversation. New York: Academic Press.

LI AN CHE (1937) "Zuni: some observations." American Anthropologist 39: 62-76.

LEVINE, R. A. (1970) "Research design in anthropological fieldwork," pp. 183-195 in R. Naroll and R. Cohen (eds.) A Handbok of Method in Cultural Anthropology. Garden City, NY: Natural History Press.

LIEBOW, E. (1967) Tally's Corner. Boston: Little, Brown.

McCARTHY, T. (1978) The Critical Theory of Jürgen Habermas. Cambridge: MIT Press.

McELROY, A. and M. A. JEZEWSKI (1984) "Boundaries and breakdowns." Presented to the meetings of the Society for Applied Anthropology, Toronto.

MEAD, M. (1970) "The art and technology of fieldwork," pp. 246-265 in R. Naroll and R. Cohen (eds.) Handbook of Method in Cultural Anthropology. Garden City, NY: Natural History Press.

———(1956) New Lives for Old. New York: Morrow.

MINSKY, M. (1975) "A framework for representing knowledge," in P. H. Winston (ed.) The Psychology of Computer Vision. New York: McGraw-Hill.

MOERMAN, M. (1969) "A little knowledge," pp. 449-469 in Stephen A. Tyler (ed.) Cognitive Anthropology. New York: Holt, Rinehart & Winston.

MOHRING, P. M. (1980) "Life, my daughter, is not the way you have it in your books." Doctoral dissertation, University of Michigan.

NAKANE, C. (1975) "Fieldwork in India—a Japanese experience," in A. Beteille and T. N. Madan (eds.) Encounter and Experience: Personal Accounts of Fieldwork. Delhi: Vikas.

NAROLL, R. (1970) "Data quality control in cross-cultural surveys," pp. 927-945 in R. Naroll and R. Cohen (eds.) A Handbook of Method in Cultural Anthropology. New York: Columbia University Press.

———and F. NAROLL (1963) "On the bias of exotic data." Man 53: 24-26.

OWUSU, M. (1978) "Ethnography of Africa: the usefulness of the useless." American Anthropologist 80: 310-334.

PANDEY, T. N. (1975) "India man among American Indians," in A. Beteille and T. N. Madan (eds.) Encounter and Experience: Personal Accounts of Fieldwork. Delhi: Vikas.

PELTO, P. J. and G. H. PELTO (1973) "Ethnography: the fieldwork enterprise," in J. H. Honigman (ed.) Handbook of Social and Cultural Anthropology. Chicago: Rand McNally.

PHILLIPS, D. C. (1976) Holistic Thought in Social Science. Stanford: Stanford University Press.

POLYA, G. (1954) Patterns of Plausible Inference. Princeton, NJ: Princeton University Press.

POWDERMAKER, H. (1966) Stranger and Friend. New York: W. W. Norton.

RABINOW, P. (1977) Reflections of Fieldwork in Morocco. Berkeley: University of California Press.

RICHARDS, A. I. (1939) "The development of field work methods in social anthropology," in F. C. Bartlett et al. (eds.) The Study of Society. London: Routledge & Kegan Paul.

RIEGER, C. J. (1975) "Conceptual memory and inference," in R. C. Shank (ed.) Conceptual Information Processing. North Holland: Elsevier.

ROSENBLATT, P. C. (1981) "Ethnographic Case Studies," in M. B. Brewer and B. E. Collins (eds.) Scientific Inquiry and Social Sciences. San Francisco: Jossey-Bass.

SCHANK, R. and ABELSON, R. (1977) Scripts, Plans, Goals and Understanding. Hillsdale, NJ: Lawrence J. Erlbaum.

SCHUTZ, A. (1970) On Phenomenology and Social Relations. Chicago: University of Chicago Press.

SIEBER, S. D. (1973) "The integration of fieldwork and survey methods." American Journal of Sociology 78: 1335-1359.

SPERBER, D. (1974) Rethinking Symbolism. Cambridge: Cambridge University Press.

TYLER, S. R. (1979) The Said and the Unsaid: Mind, Meaning and Culture. New York: Academic Press.

UCHENDU, V. A. (1970) "A Navajo Community," pp. 230-236 in R. Naroll and R. Cohen (eds.) A Handbook of Method in Cultural Anthropology. Garden City, NY: Natural History Press.

WHITEHEAD, T. L. (1984) "Breakdown, resolution, and coherence: the fieldwork experiences of a big, brown, pretty-talking man in a West Indian community. (unpublished)

WINCH, P. (1958) The Idea of a Social Science and its Relation to Philosophy. London: Routledge & Kegan Paul.

ABOUT THE AUTHOR

MICHAEL H. AGAR received his bachelor's degree in anthropology from Stanford University in 1967 and his Ph.D. from the University of California, Berkeley, in 1971. Since then, he has worked in a variety of academic and clinical settings, including the Universities of Hawaii, California, Houston, and Maryland, the NIMH Clinical Research Center in Lexington, Kentucky, and the Office of Drug Abuse Services in New York. He has done ethnographic fieldwork with villagers in South India and Austria, with urban American heroin addicts in a number of clinical and community settings, and most recently with owner-operators in the trucking industry.